Mini Farming

Grow Your Own Produce and Be Self-sufficient

(Your Ultimate Guide to Self Sufficiency Through Organic Farming)

Valerie Hurd

Published By **Phil Dawson**

Valerie Hurd

All Rights Reserved

Mini Farming: Grow Your Own Produce and Be Self-sufficient (Your Ultimate Guide to Self Sufficiency Through Organic Farming)

ISBN 978-1-77485-678-9

No part of this guidebook shall be reproduced in any form without permission in writing from the publisher except in the case of brief quotations embodied in critical articles or reviews.

Legal & Disclaimer

The information contained in this ebook is not designed to replace or take the place of any form of medicine or professional medical advice. The information in this ebook has been provided for educational & entertainment purposes only.

The information contained in this book has been compiled from sources deemed reliable, and it is accurate to the best of the Author's knowledge; however, the Author cannot guarantee its accuracy and validity and cannot be held liable for any errors or omissions. Changes are periodically made to this book. You must consult your doctor or get professional medical advice before using any of the suggested remedies, techniques, or information in this book.

Upon using the information contained in this book, you agree to hold harmless the Author from and against any damages, costs, and expenses, including any legal fees potentially resulting from the application of any of the information provided by this guide. This disclaimer applies to any damages or injury caused by the use and application, whether directly or indirectly, of any advice or information presented, whether for breach of contract, tort, negligence, personal injury, criminal intent, or under any other cause of action.

You agree to accept all risks of using the information presented inside this book. You need to consult a professional medical practitioner in order to ensure you are both able and healthy enough to participate in this program.

TABLE OF CONTENTS

Introduction 1

Chapter 1: Reasons For Indoor Gardening..3

Chapter 2: Indoor Gardening Friendly Fruits, Salad Leaves, Vegetables And Herbs 8

Chapter 3: 9 Tips For Getting The Most Effective Output 13

Chapter 4: Get Your Indoor Garden Started - Step By Step 34

Chapter 5: Square Foot Gardening - Growing Plants In Minimal Space ...48

Chapter 6: Harvesting The Fruits Of Your Work 78

Chapter 7: The Way To Acquire Space For Farming Space 83

Chapter 8: Beginning The Farm Small Farm 116

Chapter 9: The Different Types Of Gardening Based On The Space....156

Conclusion 184

Introduction

A lot of people have an enormous desire to garden however, they don't always have the time or space required to take on this passion. Indoor gardening is a great alternative for those gardening enthusiasts.

Indoor gardening is about providing optimal environmental conditions to plants in an enclosed space to allow them to grow quickly. This kind of gardening can be difficult because it needs an extensive amount of maintenance. But when you have the right type of direction and advice it can be pleasant and easy.

In the beginning you can plant herbaceous plants and other leafy ones in your garden indoors. They're a little easier to cultivate than plants like beet and potatoes. But, with appropriate experience it is possible to grow difficult plants.

Square foot gardening however is done outside. However, the basic principles are similar because they are about making the most effective use of a small area. When you are trying to grow food for your table, there appears to be a widespread belief out there that says you require an extensive garden to be able to grow it successfully.

However, this is not the case. All you require is a patch that is about one-quarter of the width of a typical door to produce sufficient vegetables that can feed an average family of four.

The most effective method is to plan it properly and utilize the space available for the most effective outcomes.

The square foot garden is a simple method of growing a range of vegetables. All you have to do is divide the area you have into sections that are approximately one foot square and then plant the appropriate plants.

This book will show how to do it right the first time around.

Chapter 1: Reasons For Indoor Gardening

Who Does Indoor Gardening Appeal To?

There are numerous reasons to get started in indoor gardening, ranging including the lack of space in apartment buildings to cultivating one's favourite crop even when it's not in season.

Apartment dwellers tend to favor gardening indoors due to the space limitations, however there are many others who might be attracted to this kind of gardening too.

For instance, older people are another population that are attracted by gardening. For many elderly gardening outdoors in the heat of the day can be too strenuous however, having the use of indoor pots for their favourite plants is easier to maintain.

Families with large families are another type that are attracted to gardening indoors. The cost of vegetables can be quite high and you may not have time to maintain an extensive garden. A couple of vegetables could be a huge boost to your budget.

The absence of Outdoor Space

If you're limited with outdoor space, or in an apartment with no balcony and a garden, outdoor gardening might be the best choice for you.

If you reside in apartments that have balconies space outdoor, indoor gardening becomes more simple for you since all you need to do indoor gardening is sunshine.

Light sources could be via windows or from the light of an outdoor balcony.

Taste and Quality

Take a taste of the tomatoes you buy in the grocery store as well as the ones you can find at vineyards. You'll be able to distinguish between the mass production and your garden's production.

Typically, in the case of mass production the vegetables are harvested before maturation and placed in storage cold. From there, the veggies are then transported across the world. Since the plants aren't suitable for ripening in the sunlight, they are more likely to be less tasty.

This is the reason why often, you will find that the purchased vegetables are tasteless and less fresh. This can affect the quality of the fruits and vegetables that make it to your home.

Indoor gardening makes sure that you make use of ripe fruit and vegetables, and you ensure that you get the best nutritional components that are present in the fruits and vegetables. You can pick them whenever you require them and consume them fresh without cold storage whatsoever.

Organic and Natural

If you're growing your own crops you are aware of the types of pesticides, fertilizers, as well as organic manures have been utilized in order to achieve the desired crop. You don't need to apply harmful chemicals in order to ensure a healthy crop, which means you can ensure that your own crops are organic. This gives you the peace of mind that you're eating a healthy foods.

Cost Factor

Imagine that you have to prepare Russian salad and you have all the ingredients you need on your balcony. The good thing is that you won't have to spend a cent or go through the hassle of going to the store and buying the ingredients.

The fruits and vegetables can be expensive, particularly when they are not in the season. Gardening indoors can help you understand that growing your own vegetables is cost-effective. In addition, you will produce crops that aren't readily available in the supermarkets since they aren't in season.

When there are national emergencies, the cost of food can increase by a third. In times of emergency knowing that you have your own garden that is in the field can make a huge difference in cash.

Self-Satisfaction

Indoor gardening can give a feeling of achievement for you. It is essential to devote your energy, time and care to the plants. They require an enormous amount of attention however, when you finally get results in the form of mature vegetables and fruits The feeling of satisfaction that you'll feel is beyond words.

The plants in your home can create a peaceful display. Being in the natural world can be extremely relaxing after a tiring day working.

They also are incredibly efficient in removing carbon dioxide from the air that they require for breathing. They emit oxygen in this process.

Cleaner air is a good thing and, if you're into it, you can select plants with an appealing aroma. The basil pot is a good example. It has a fresh, herbal smell and leaves are great for cooking.

Chapter 2: Indoor Gardening Friendly Fruits, Salad Leaves, Vegetables And Herbs

There are a variety of fruits or vegetables as well as herbs you can plant in your home. Below is an overview of the best options to get going, however we suggest you try alternative options as well.

The chapter 3 will walk through the steps to finding the ideal location and how to create the perfect environment for growth. Then, in Chapter 4, we guide you through the process of planting.

At present, however it is possible to expand the next.

Peppers

There are some tips for making peppers grow successfully in your house. The main requirement to grow peppers is a warm, sunny location. It is necessary to establish at the minimum of 75 degrees C temperature for peppers to thrive.

Smaller peppers like Peppadews or Chili peppers can easily be grown in your home. Peppers can also take up lots of space, therefore it is best to make use of a four to five gallon container.

For faster results, it is possible to use seeds in place of the pepper seeds. It is important to water the plants regularly sufficient to ensure that the soil remains wet, but not too that it becomes completely soaked.

Green onion

The green onions are simple to cultivate. Simply take one stem of green onion along with a few roots, and cut it one inch away from the bottom. Then place it in a glass filled with water. Allow it to develop until it's at a minimum doubled in size and produced a plethora of roots. Cutting off the green top will allow you to cook with it.

It's a win-win for everyone, and Instead of throwing out the top parts to the trash like you would normally and wasting them, you can grow your own onions instead. If the plant is big enough, you can transplant to a container filled with adequate soil and

enough water to make sure the soil is moist.
Leave it in sunlight and observe it grow.

Basil

Basil has a lovely scent and is delicious. It is possible to sprinkle basil over your tomato salad, Mediterranean dishes or on any sauce, and it will enhance the taste of your dish. While you can purchase dried basil, fresh kind is the best choice.

Basil is available in a range of leaf sizes and types. It is also possible to purchase the purple-colored basil.

This plant will require full sun for around 4 hours every day. It is most productive when it is in the to the south. If you notice that the basil plant has turned limp, then it is time to you should water it. If you notice flowers emerging from the plant, then cut the stems. The presence of the flowers could cause the leaves to taste bitter.

In addition to basil, you can cultivate rosemary, mint, and sage, the same manner.

Tomato

They require adequate light to thrive, therefore you'll need to set up the ideal conditions inside your home for them to thrive. It is essential to use an ample pot and select a cultivar that produces smaller tomatoes, like cherry or Roma tomatoes.

Full-sized tomatoes can technically be grown, however they need lots of space and you'll need to find a way to hold the main stems. Use smaller varieties to get the most benefit.

It is important to position the tomato in an area that receives the most sunlight. The plants should be facing in a the south and make sure that the container is rotated frequently. So that every one of areas of the pot are getting equally much sunlight.

Lettuce

It is only available in the summer, but when you grow indoors you can have salads even during winter. It requires a lot of sunlight , so it is best to place it where it can receive the most sunlight, even in the winter time.

Place lettuce in a large container that is as big as half a gallon capacity. You can also grow Microgreens and Swiss Chard in the same manner in your own home.

Parsley

Parsley requires sunshine that is direct for approximately 8 hours per day on a regular basis. Parsley requires a container with a depth of about 10 inches and 18 inches wide in order for it to flourish. The plant should be watered regularly, but allow the soil to dry between every watering.

There are two types of parsley: curly leaf parsley or the flat leaf variety. The flat leaves tend to be more delicious and are suitable for use to garnish virtually any food.

It's not easy to cultivate parsley directly from seed , so begin with seedlings.

Chapter 3: 9 Tips For Getting The Most Effective Output

Find the Right Space

Indoor gardening can be effective only when you can provide a suitable environment that encourages plants to thrive. It is entirely dependent on the amount of space you wish to devote to indoor gardening in your home. You can put your own table or bench for the garden or put your plants on the windowsill.

To get the most out of your garden space you can think about using shelves similar to the one shown above. Or, go for an open-air bookcase, or a set of stackable shelves. Whatever you decide to use be sure that every and every shelf receives sufficient sunlight.

In the next section in the next chapter, we'll walk through the step-by-step process of creating the first garden in your home. Before we can get there but, it's an excellent idea to know some of the fundamentals.

The space you choose to plant indoors also depends on the amount and position of windows in your home. Most often, east and west facing windows are the best to grow indoors. They get the most sunlight and help the growth of plants. This is especially crucial for plants like tomatoes and lettuce which require more light.

Don't start your garden indoors in a damp and cool space in your house, such as the attic or garage. Most of the time, the temperature in these areas isn't enough and can hinder the development that your backyard. In some cases it is possible that the cold area could even cause the death of the plants.

Avoid areas that are directly underneath an air vent or a fan. A lot of air circulation can dry out plants and cause damage to the plants. Also, you can use a hanging planters that give an updated style to your house and can also solve the problem of a limited space.

Choose the Right Kind Of Light Source

Light is the most important requirement for any plant's development. Plants require light to photosynthesis. If plants don't receive enough sunlight, they will not develop properly and won't be able to grow vegetables and fruits in the way that is desired.

Every plant requires at least four hours of sun, that they may not receive during winter or rainy times. Additionally, if you have shelves, sunlight may not penetrate the lower shelves in a proper manner. These are the main reasons that you should set up artificial lights for your plants.

It is simple to make fake lighting to plants. An average garden size of 18" 18" x 18" requires at least 100 watts of artificial lighting. It is essential to adhere to certain guidelines to obtain the best lighting that your garden needs.

The plants absorb only a particular wavelength of light. The one that is the same light wavelength. You'll need a grow light source that matches what wavelength sunlight has. Light bulbs that are typical are not appropriate for indoor gardening .

Every plant produces a unique kind of hormone called florigen, which triggers the process of flowering and budding in plants. A typical long-day plant will require approximately 16 hours of sunlight to create this hormone and a small one will require around 12 hours to complete the process to take place. Be sure to know your plants very well and provide them with the right amount of sunlight. If a plant is exposed to too much light in a short time and the hormone that is responsible for flowering or budding is destroyed.

Also, you must consider the distance that you position the lights. If the lights are placed close in proximity to plants, they may even ignite plants' leaves.

To determine if plants are getting the right amount of light, look at the color, size and size of the stem of the plant. If the leaf's size is tiny and the stem is thin and the leaves have a light yellow or green color It means the plant isn't getting enough light.

The spiral CFL bulbs make up the simplest grow lights are available at affordable costs. It can serve as a substitute for sunshine for a short period of time and is ideal on cloudy days. If you want to purchase a top-quality grow lightsthat are able to keep your plants in good shape for longer durations and that are adequate enough to cover the entire landscape, you'll have to invest more.

Metal halide, high-pressure sodium and compact fluorescent light bulbs have higher efficiency over CFL bulbs. Compact fluorescent lamps are small in terms of size, but they are bright in the natural world. Metal Halides reflect blue-white light which is ideal for the growth of green crops. High-pressure sodium emits orange-red light, which is ideal for budding and flowering.

Keep Growth-friendly environmental conditions

There are a variety of conditions in the environment, such as humidity, temperature etc. that are essential to ensure the proper development of an indoor plant. These aspects will vary according to the kind of garden you'd like to establish and the kinds of plants you would like to cultivate within your backyard.

Typically, a temperature between 65 and 75 degrees F is suitable for all types of plants, with the buffer of either plus or less than 10-degree F. If the temperature goes beyond the limit mentioned, your garden plants could have weak and tiny leaves. If the temperature range is below the specified limit and your plants aren't able to tolerate it, they could be covered in yellow leaves and may shed leaves before the beginning of the autumn season.

The temperature range described above isn't ideal for the general environment of your house. To achieve a equilibrium between your living and garden area, it is possible to place electric mats on the bottom of your pots. They'll heat the pots from the bottom , and help regulate the soil's temperature in the way you want.

In addition to temperatures, you're also expected to keep the humidity levels of your garden. The winter months are much more dry than summer, and maintaining an environment that is humid in winter is a difficult task. If you're supplying an artificial lighting source, the challenge is made more difficult.

There are several ways to check if your plants are receiving the right humidity levels or not. Examine the tips of plant leaves. If they begin to turn brown, this indicates that the plant isn't getting enough humidity. Also, you will notice that the plants are shed excessive leaves, and they'll start to appear swollen slowly.

There are several natural methods to boost the humidity of the garden. Make a tray of water and place it in your garden. Place lava rocks inside the tray. They increases the area that water evaporates. More water will raise the humidity levels in the air.

Plants should be placed closer to one another so that they aren't burdened by creating a moist and humid environments over a wider area. For a decent quantity of humidity, you can make use of an artificial humidifier to provide a favorable environment for your plants.

Alternately, you can create a miniature-greenhouse appearance by using cloches, or a clear cover that covers that top layer of pot.

Pick Your Container Carefully

The choice of the container is based heavily on the kind of plants you're looking for as well as their need for humidity and the amount of space needed to cultivate them. There is a wide range of containers made from ceramic, plastic and various other materials. To add a touch of uniqueness you can also make use of gorgeous plastic bottles. You can make your own containers out of terracotta since they look stunning. You can also look into other alternatives like old tins or even old tins. Make sure they've been properly cleaned first.

Usually, a large container that is deep is best for plants since it will have enough room for its roots to develop into the earth. It also guarantees that the soil will retain the moisture for a long duration. So, you'll be able to skip every day watering, and your plants will remain in perfect health.

Be sure that your pots have drainage holes in the bottom. Place your pots on trays so that plants are able to use water that flows through the soil and into the tray. It is also possible to place rocks to the bottom of the pots before you plant the soil in order to help drain the water to the fullest extent possible.

To keep a decent amount of water in your plants, it is recommended to use plastic containers. If you are a fan of wooden containers, ensure that you use containers constructed of redwood or cedar since they are resistant to rot. Don't use containers that were treated with any type of chemical. This could be extremely hazardous for your plants and you may end up growing poisonous fruit and vegetables.

A good soil is important.

Do not simply pull out the soil that is on the soil outside and then apply it to indoor gardening. This soil may contain many weeds, insects and pests, as well as the soil could be extremely heavy. You'll need an appropriate soil mix for an indoor landscape. The most fundamental characteristic of a healthy growing soil is the fact that it drains well and is flexible in the natural environment. The soil must also contain enough organic matter that it can store water and nutrients effectively.

It is essential to match the kind of soil with the kind of plant you're cultivating. For instance, nasturtiums prefer soil that is less fertile. If the soil isn't healthy, you'll get lots of lush, green leaves, but less flowers.

In the majority of instances, though you'll need the best quality of potter's soil. In nature, plant roots are able to spread further to obtain nutrients. In pots, they don't have that option.

You can purchase organic mix from stores or make it yourself. In order to make this, you'll require soil worms, forest humus as well as sandy loam.

Growing In Water

If you don't want to invest time and effort in creating soil, then you could utilize hydroponics. It is a method in which the plants are grown in water and get the nutrients that are easily available on the market. This means that plants can be grown without soil.

The principal function for soil is the fact that it stores nutrients and supplies it to the plant's roots so that they can expand. Hydroponics allows you to give the nutrients you need directly to your plants. As you can see in the image above, it appears similar to a typical soil installation. There are numerous advantages to hydroponics aside of the fact they're readily accessible. Your plants will develop rapidly, perhaps up to 50% faster since plants are able to access food and water quickly and effortlessly. It also provides the plants with a healthy environment and ultimately, increases the chances of obtaining an efficient and healthy crop. If any plant is affected, it will be at a safe distance and your garden will not be damaged.

Additionally, you can increase your growth in a smaller area.

When you utilize hydroponics the roots of the plants can grow in different directions without following one path. This means you can even use small containers since the roots of your plants won't grow in the deepest part of your container. The plants you choose to plant will show signs of dehydration since they'll begin to slide down. The plants won't die in a hurry, and you'll be able to keep them alive.

If you're taking the path of hydroponic gardening make sure your coconut fibers and pebbles for hydroponics because they require to support the roots during the beginning stages. It is also necessary to provide plenty of manures and fertilizers since your plants will obtain nutrition from the two sources just.

We will not discuss this issue here because it's a bit difficult to set up. However we suggest you investigate more about it.

Aquaponics is a different offshoot of this method where you grow fish in water. The idea is that fish will supply the plant with the nutrients they require by excreting waste and the plants will supply the fish with the nutrition they require to develop. This is, of course, quite complicated, and we will not discuss it here.

Correct Use of Fertilizer

You'll need to ensure that you are using fertilizers and provide them in an adequate quantities since you're conducting indoor gardening. Your plants won't be able to get any other nutrients. There are many fertilizers on the market and you are able to select depending on your personal preferences.

There is even compost that you can use to make soil healthy and rich, which eventually aids your plants to grow effectively. Before choosing a specific kind of compost, ensure that you're not planting plants that need low-quality soil. There are some species of wildflowers that need poor soil quality to thrive. If you make use of compost to grow these plants, you may cause harm to them.

If you've got some space at house, there are plenty of small composting systems that need just one activator, and then a bin to keep the waste. These are a useful accessory for the gardener who is at home.

Keep in mind that you should only add organic kitchen waste such as vegetable peels, vegetable waste, etc. It is not advisable to add cooked fooditems, dairy, or meat of any kind , or you risk the likelihood of foodborne bacteria settling within the waste.

Also, be aware of the non-acidic and acidic requirements of your selected plants. Make sure you are feeding your soil with different fertilizers that are compatible with the requirements specific to your plants.

Keep an eye at the quantity of fertilizer you give your plants. Over-use of fertilizer can also be detrimental. The extra fertilizers can create the appearance of salt in containers, which could cause fire to your plants. If you observe any of these structures, it is best to change your containers or wash them and keep an eye on the fertilizer you use.

Organic Foods are important for indoor Plants

Other than fertilisers, there's many other ways to supply nutrients to your plants. It is possible to use organic ingredients such as fruit and vegetable peels to give your plants a boost.

There are some plants such as rosebushes that require lots of potassium to flourish. To give your plants an additional dosage of potassium make use of banana peels. Peels of bananas are rich in concentration of potassium. You can throw out bananas and place its peels in the soil in which you plan to plant rose bush. The potassium content contained in the peel will aid blooming roses throughout the year.

Another natural ingredient that is beneficial is eggshells. Eggshells are a great source of nutrients for soil and assist plants grow like tomatoes and pepper tremendously. Eggshells are a great source of nutrition to plants over all of the season.

Rinse them well before crushing the eggs prior to digging them into the soil , or making compost from them. You can also put them inside prior to planting your crops. Sprinkle them over the soil and they'll be effective.

With eggshells, it is possible to get delicious and tasty vegetables and fruits out of your garden. There's another benefit of eggshells. They're a great natural barrier due to the fact that their edges are sharp. They can stop any type of insect, such as the slug from getting into your plants.

Don't throw away your coffee grinds - they are extremely beneficial to the soil. The following soil mix can help you provide your plants with the nutrients they require

and will be helpful when you have pets that attempt to eat eggshells:
* Eggshells crushed
* Coffee grounds
* Banana peels

Place all the ingredients in your blender or food processor and blend until it is fine. Then it can be swiftly and easily disposed of over your garden, or added into the compost.

To deter small animals from your outdoor garden, it is possible to sprinkle soap flakes around the garden. This will keep them from entering your garden. You could also use hair of a person and urine from predators to keep them out. To deter slugs from your garden, sprinkle a few pennies on your garden. Metal is a fantastic repellent for snails.

You should provide the right amount of sunlight

It is also subjective and every plant requires a different amount of sun. Some require complete sunlight, and others need only partial sun and others need shade. This is an important aspect which will determine how healthy your plants will develop.

Before you purchase plants, you'll be required to examine the entire area you are considering to plant indoors. It is essential to know which areas will receive the most sunshine throughout the day. Be sure to select a place with patches of complete sunshine, a few areas of shade and areas that are between. This will increase the variety of plants you are able to plant there.

There are some plants that thrive exceptionally well in shaded environments These plants are ideal in indoor gardens. If you notice the plant is becoming thin and pointed toward the light, this means that the plant needs more sun. Alter the position of the plant right away.

It is also possible to rotate your plants when they are in sunlight or in shaded areas so that they are getting everything in an the right quantity. It will make sure that your plants receive sunlight in every direction. The plants that are planted in tiny pots already have consumed plenty of sunlight. Give the plants a break by placing them in an area which gets shade during the afternoon.

Water Plants Properly

The importance of watering is a key element for indoor gardens. It is essential to supply just the proper amount of water to your plants, not too much or too little. Both situations can harm your plants. Don't believe that excessive water is beneficial for all plants. In fact, excessive watering causes rot to set in. Plants that were grown in pots require more water than those that are grown outdoors in natural conditions.

This is due to the fact that in nature, plants has access to a more extensive layer of soil. In a pot, this tiny amount of soil is dried out extremely quickly.

There's a simple way to figure out the best time and amount to be watering your plants. Put your finger in the soil , about 1 inch. If you feel that there is a dryness in the soil, you are able to give your plants a good watering. The water should be drained until it begins to drain through the gap on the base in the container.

In the event that you find that your plants' leaves are turning brown, this means that your plants require additional water. If the leaves and flowers on your plant are falling off prematurely this means you're lacking a sufficient water supply. If your plants stopped growing earlier than they should and are discolored or are wilting from the stem It is a sign that you're watering them to excessively.

There are succulents that look like pants that naturally thrive in dry areas. These plants require less water. The winter plants are another type that need less water. Additionally, seedlings require more water compared to mature plants. Seedlings are in their growing phase , and require a greater amount of water. Till you see the first real set of leaves appearing on your seedling, just a couple of inches above the soil, make sure to keep your seeds in a moist place. Make sure that your seeds don't dry before they begin to sprout.

Your water's quality consume is another aspect. Certain plants, like orchids that require good water quality. If you give them drinking water from the tap, they may be damaged due to their sensitivity to the chemicals in tap water. In the case of such plants it is possible to utilize spring water or distilled water.

There are even containers that can determine the water requirements on their own. These containers are available in a range of shapes and colors. When a plant is placed in these pots, the containers will be aware of when plants require water and will drink water accordingly.

Chapter 4: Get Your Indoor Garden Started - Step By Step

First Step: How Are you going to grow?
It's important to decide first because it will provide you with some idea about the type of container you should use as well as the most suitable place to put the plant.
It is likely, for example, that you'd require a bigger pot for growing carrots than you would grow lettuce. It's not true. While lettuce is producing its crop above the soil, its root system sinks pretty deep too.

Find out which root system the plant you are considering is growing in. If it has a tap root similar to a lettuce, it will require a bigger pot. If it is tubers, similar to the carrot similar to a carrot, the same is true. If it has fibrous roots it is possible to use smaller pots.
Once you've found out what the roots do you will also have to figure out the amount of space each plant requires to develop and how quickly they expand.

For instance plant some carrots amongst the lettuce, and then pull the carrots out when they're still small so you can harvest baby carrots.

You can also add radishes between your lettuce. They are fast-growing enough to allow harvesting before they become a serious issue for the roots of your lettuce.

Furthermore, since most of the plants here are below ground, you can fill all every inch of space in between of your lettuce and harvest the highest quantity of crops in one pot.

Consider looking into family heirlooms which are smaller than the norm.

For a general guideline to follow, you should choose an area with a minimum of a foot deep if you're cultivating a crop that has tap roots.

This is the Quick Cheat Option

Did you remember that you could cultivate green onions if you cut one inch off of the top with the roots still attached and then place the onion in water.

You can make similar things with regular onions too. But you don't require one inch of onion. Simply cut off the portion that has the root and put it in the water.

It will not be long before it begins to develop a lot of roots, then it begins to grow the stalk. If you notice it is beginning to rise - and it appears like the rings are growing in one place and it's time to plant the onion.

Step Two Step Two: Preparing the Pot

If you are aware of the kind of plant you have and what you want to grow, you can select the perfect pot or container , for your plant. It must have at least one hole punched into the bottom to ensure that the water drains out. Pick a saucer that matches, or else you'll need to take it out to the sink each time you fill it with water.

Find out the perfect soil mix for the particular plant you own. Make sure you have the right mix.

Prepare your pot now.

Begin by laying down the stone or pebbles. The layer should be approximately an inch in thickness. This is to aid in draining of the plant. This also aids in preventing root rot since your plant's roots will be in a position to take all water away.

It ought to look something like this:

Step Three: Plant Your Plant

Then you can plant the seedling or seedling of onion we talked about.

Many people are unsure whether it's best to go with seeds or seedlings. It will depend on what you're planting. For instance, carrots should be planted as close to where they will develop from seeds.

In general, the plant with taproot system is not one that wants to be perturbed. It is possible to do this if you've got the seedlings of lettuce or carrots so long as they're not allowed to become well established before they can be transplanted.

Roots that have fibrous structures are more easy to transfer.

The advantage of beginning with seeds is that you are able to observe the entire process of growth unfold from start to end. It'll take longer and may require more effort.

Seeds should be kept in a moist environment as described earlier. Additionally, if you've sewn very fine seeds, as in the case of carrots, you must reduce the size of the seedlings that are springing up to allow enough space for the tubers to grow.

There is there is a chance that seeds won't sprout in the absence of the conditions suitable. If you aren't sure what the seedling ought to look like, you might encounter issues with weeds which you aren't aware of.

If you are a beginner It is best to start by planting a seedling. In the beginning, it will save you the effort and time of taking care of the seeds that do not develop. In addition it reduces the period between harvesting and planting.

Perhaps you just require a couple of plants. A package of basil seeds for instance, is not enough for a single plant. Seeds do go "off" over time. The more old the seed the less likely it will grow.

It's time to plant again, now. If you're planting seeds, the seed packet will provide an idea of the distance they should be spread out, and the depth at which to plant them.

In the case of most seeds, you can just place your fingers in the soil around one inch deep, then place the seed in the soil, and then cover it with. For extremely fine seeds like carrots, you'll create an elongated furrow, then sprinkle seeds over it, then cover them with.

If you wish to stimulate seeds to germinate earlier it is possible to soak them in water that is tepid for a few hours prior to planting them. Be aware that tepid is not boiling hot or hot.

If you're making seedlings, the process is the same, with one exception: you'll need to dig the hole. The hole must be large enough that the roots fit inside comfortably and that you can make an oval shape around the exterior part of your plant.

This "saucer" can help bring water closer to the root to where it is required.

Remove the plant gently from the bag or container and then place it in the hole you made to place it in. Incorporate the soil with it. Allow some room to make the saucer. Tamp down the soil to ensure that it's firm, so that the plant will be secured.

The next step is similar regardless of whether the seeds or plants. The pot should be given a generous amount of water. It is important to ensure that the water reaches the bottom, and that your soil has been completely wet. It isn't necessary to do this repeatedly, however it's crucial to do it first time.

If you've planted seeds, it's finished. Remove the saucer from under the plant when it has drained and make plans to water your plant the following day, around the same time.

If you've planted seedlings, it is important to ensure whether the plant is solidly in its the correct position. If it is not, you can tamp the soil and think about adding soil. If you decide to do this, re-water.

After everything is fine After everything is okay, pour the water from the saucer on the bottom.

If the pots aren't in their final positions then move them to the correct position now.

Step Four: Water Your Plant

Self-Watering System

If you're concerned about not being able to water your plants, simple self-watering systems like the one below may be the solution. It should be an herb with fibrous roots, not tap roots.

The only thing you need to do is grab an enormous soda bottle and cut the bottle in half. The aim is to make that the bottle's neck extend just above the bottom that is inside the bottle. The lid should be removed and discarded. the lid.

Join the two pieces in the manner shown above. Thread a length of cotton string around the neck of the bottle to ensure that there are around the size of two to three wires at the bottle's bottom and also that you have one long piece of string that extends across the bottle's opening. Secure this string at the moment.

Make sure to fill the top of your bottle up with water. The amount should be sufficient so to ensure that the neck is nearly touch the top of the bottle. Prepare the upper portion similar to in a pot. Make use of stones in the neck that are too small to fall completely through.

There is only a couple of less than an inch like in the typical pot. The rest of the pot with soil and place the plants in.

Unclip the string and move it with care to the middle of the plant. What happens is that the string draws up water through osmosis, when it is moist. The plant then gets enough water that it needs at the time it is in need of it.

You might need to refill with water once in a while time, but the plant is able to do the rest.

Normal Watering

How much water a plant requires will depend on the stage it is in its growth cycle as well as the amount of water it prefers. Investigate your plants to learn more about what they prefer.

The main thing is that seeds must always remain humid. This typically means that they are watered every day until the first leaves have begun to sprout out.

Then, determine the time to water them by looking at the content of moisture in the soil. Use the simple test of your fingers we discussed before in this book to determine whether or not you have to water your plant.

When watering, it's recommended to know what the plant likes. Tomatoes, for instance, don't like having the water dripping off their leaves. Likewise, If you spray their leaves they will be affected by Blight.

To water a tomato, as well as many other veggies it is recommended to soak as close to the ground as you can without getting your leaves wet.

Some plants such as orchids, are not able to stand with its roots being in water. It is best to mist them, then remove any water.

For plants that prefer more humidity such as the eggplant, misting your plant could aid in creating a more humid atmosphere and could be a more effective method to water.

It is recommended to water your plants around the same time throughout the day. It is recommended to water them in the morning so that they can get the water they require for the coming next day. Be mindful not to splash water onto the leaves, and ensure you be sure to water them correctly when it's sunny.

The water that falls on leaves may cause leaves to become burnt in the sun. A moderate amount of water will do nothing more than move the root closer so that sunlight can harm them.

If you're required to water your plants at night it's fine but make sure to do this prior to the temperature dropping too much.

Step Five Step Five: Feeding Your Plant

There's only so much nutrition in the pot that your plant can consume. If you want your plant to flourish it is essential to nourish it appropriately. When it is time for flowers the plant requires additional nutrients, particularly when it is producing fruit.

Review the rules for each specific plant.

Step Six: Monitor Its Progression

It is recommended to check your plant every second or third day , to check if it requires water. Also you should evaluate its overall state of health.

Even if you've got little knowledge of plants, it is relatively easy to tell whether the plant is flourishing or not.

Dry, wet leaves may indicate that the place is hot or you've not given sufficient water. A limp, flaccid plant may indicate that you have excessive water.

We covered these signs earlier in the chapter, but we'll go over them in greater detail in the next chapter.

Now you are able to turn the plant around a quarter of a circle each when you inspect it If you'd like. This will make sure that growth is evenly distributed throughout.

In time the plant could become too big to fit in the pot. If you have a plant that is growing quickly, you should anticipate having to repotte every year or more. Take your cues from the plant's characteristics - certain plants, such as orchids, don't like being repotted.

Sometimes it may be essential - if the plant is roots bound, its growth will be severely slowed and it will be more likely to develop any kind of disease.

Seventh Step: The Harvest

The time to harvest or if you pick in the first place depends on the type of plant you've planted. If you plant plants solely to bloom, taking out the dead plants after the flowers have gone out is the only harvesting you have to accomplish.

If you're growing vegetables, harvest them when they are mature. For carrots and onions typically, this is the time when the green tops start slowing down.

If you have fruiting vegetables or trees, you'll follow the shape of your fruit. If the plant does not produce yield fruit, or the fruit is thin or distorted this means something in the mix of nutrients isn't right.

Herbs are among the most enjoyable potted plants. When it comes to herbs such as basil and mint it is recommended to harvest them frequently to encourage growth. You can try pinching off the crown leaves from each stem. If you don't then the plant will become in a scraggly and leggy manner. If you do cut the crowns the plant will spread out beautifully.

Chapter 5: Square Foot Gardening - Growing Plants In Minimal Space

They were created to be outdoors. Therefore, should you desire the most optimal results from vegetables and fruits the outdoor garden is the best option.

There is no need for an enormous area to get started A patch that is about equal to the width of an doorway is enough to plant a large vegetable patch. It's an issue of picking the appropriate vegetables and the ideal place.

Pick A Place
Location, location, location. This is as vital in landscaping as with real estate. It is best to select the area closest to the house to allow you to more manage your garden.

Find a place with a lot of shade inside your backyard. You don't want your seedlings to be competing with the soaring winds such as. If you are experiencing problems with wind it's a good idea to put up an wind break of some sort.

Certain shrubs can perform their job well However, don't put close to the place where your garden will go. They should allow you to shut the wind, but not compete with your garden for water.

The space should be adequately ventilated. Although it's not the best idea to put your garden close to a wall which bakes in the sun for all day, it's an ideal idea to supply the garden with some shields against the wind . Your plants will do better if they don't get affected by windy conditions all day long.

Pick a comfortable location within the gardens.

It is not important how the soil looks the area you will plant your garden as you'll be making raised beds, so select an area that is suitable for you.

Vegetables require at least 4 to 6 hours of sunlight a day, so ensure that the spot you select receives plenty of sun. Select a place that gets the most sunlight in the morning feasible as it will be more beneficial for your plants.

If you're concerned about your plants frying during the summer, you could build a shade structure for them too.

It's recommended to have a water source close by so that you are able to swiftly provide water to your plants in the event of a need. Be careful not to place your bed in a place that is that is prone to flooding. Also, ensure that it is located in an area that is well-drained.

Beware of areas with bushes or trees close by due to two reasons. First of all, they'll shade the area. And, thirdly the roots of these trees are also looking for water and nutrients. They will form a line to your raised bed, making it difficult for your plants to grow. If you are left with no other option then you can add a base of solid plywood to your frame , so that your bed does not have interaction with soil. It is necessary to drill drainage holes in the base.

How to build an elongated Foot Garden Bed

Materials

* 4x4 feet pieces of lumber at minimum 6 inches wide with a thickness of 1 inch
* 6 x 4-foot wood laths

Equal amounts of vermiculite, garden compost and peat moss

* Decking screws at minimum 2 inches long
- A drill for power
* One roll of string
* A tape or ruler is a good way to measure.
* Weed cloth, Tarp newspaper, cardboard or Tarp and weed cloth will withstand all elements much better. Newspaper and cardboard will degrade however, they are relatively cheap.

Tips

Choose a lumber that will stand up well in the face of the elements. The cost of hardwood is higher but it lasts longer than soft wood such as pine. It shouldn't treat or be coated in any manner when you grow food. The chemicals contained in treated wood could be absorbed into the soil, and then into your vegetables and other vegetables. Make sure the hardware store cuts the wood into the proper lengths that you need.

Make sure the beds are four feet by four feet. you are able to add additional beds in the future but this is an acceptable size.

Directions

Making the frame for your bed is very simple Just make sure you make use of a sturdy smooth surface to ensure that the bed is straight and stable. Set up the boards and turn the corners in such a way that you're left with the shape of a square. Drill holes for the screws at the top of each corner. Place these in the basic frame.

Once the basic design is in place after which you are now able to drill the remaining holes. Three screws are required to fix every corner. You'll end up with something similar to this:

If you wish for your wood to be durable you can rub it with Linseed oil. It is crucial to choose untreated wood since the chemicals found in treated wood can be absorbed into the soil, and then contaminate your garden. If you'd like to paint the top and outside of the frame, but ensure that the interior is free of any contaminants.

Wood is the cheapest material, however, you could choose to, construct a sturdy frame from mortar and bricks.

Set your frame on the appropriate place and check how it appears. Be sure it's solid against the ground, and then place it on the grass cloth/tarp or even cardboard.

If you're using the tarp method, you'll have to take the additional step of creating drainage holes within it from time to time. The next image will help you make these holes.

The inside should be filled with soil. Then take each piece and divide the squares into pieces that are about a foot wide and foot long. Lay the string across the top so you can see the layout that will look like prior to connecting the laths.

If you're happy with your grid, then begin to put up your grid. Lay out each lath in 1-

foot intervals across the breadth and length of the square. You can have three layers across the length of the square as well as three laths running across the length of the rectangle.

Drill holes at the points where the laths meet each other and screw them in securely.

Also create holes where frames and laths intersect to attach the grid onto the frame.

Repeat this process until you've got the amount of frames you would like and then set them out to test what they look like. Your final piece should look like this.

If you're planning to make several beds, it is best to leave some space between them to ensure you can move around and explore every inch of your garden. It is possible to set the beds up in such a way that they turn into some sort of decorative element as shown below.

Making a frame by this method saves you from having to do a lot of work. It's much easier than digging out soil. It will save you many back-breaking hours because you are putting in the correct soil from the start.

There is no reason to be concerned about weeding as they will be covered by the very first layer of tarp/weed paper or even cardboard.

The garden's higher level will help to avoid excessive stooping.

Soil

The secret to success in gardening square feet is to find the perfect balance in soil. It's initially a small amount of effort to get it right, but once you've got the right balance, you don't need to think about it ever again.

Begin by gathering all the elements to make your soil. You will require equal amounts of peat moss, compost and vermiculite. Be aware that equal quantities in this case refer to the volume in each of the ingredients, but not necessarily weight.

1. Compost

Compost can be described as Mother Nature's Vitamin preparation for plants. The well-balanced compost is a source of nutrients to help support healthy plants and is simple to use. It holds water, but it doesn't become saturated and is still flexible and pliable, and top of all homemade compost is the most effective.

It is easy to compost and could take up to two weeks, if you do it done correctly. A composting container makes the entire process simpler however, you could also create a composting heap in the event that you would like to. It's important to ensure enough moisture, mass and air circulation in order to feed the bacteria that are responsible for decomposition.

If you're looking to get results quickly make sure you mix in as many different types of vegetation as you can. Mix with grass clippings (dried) vegetable peels dry leaves, dry peels and any other plant you might think of.

It is also possible to add eggshells or tea leaves but don't add any dairy or meat, or you could draw vermin.

It is important to ensure that all of the matter that is going into compost is broken into small pieces. The smaller the pieces, the more quickly it will break down.

Check that you have a pile that is moist but not wet or dry, but rather damp.

Make sure to turn the pile every day to see the most effective results.

If you're interested building your own composting drum . an aluminum trash container with the lid that is tight and has holes punched into it that let air to enter is a cost-effective option to create your own compost bin.

If you're looking for results that are quick Mix everything well before adding it to the mix.

The process can be kicked off by adding manure, but ensure that it's from animals that do not consume meat, or you could risk getting the compost contaminated.

To ensure the optimal balance of nutrients from a compost pile, it is recommended to include at least five distinct ingredients. This creates a rich compost that is enriched with a wide range of nutrients and minerals.

Another option that works for those who wish to let nature run its course is to make an area that is about two inches deep. In this, you can put the kitchen waste we discussed gardening clippings, the garden and at times you can also put some newspaper.

Every now and then. Add a few inches of soil to the top, and then add make sure to water. It will take longer than a composting pile garbage bin but won't require turning too often. The benefit is that when the compost is broken down, it creates an abundant loamy soil which will fill the pit, and over the course of a year, around the time, you'll have the perfect place to plant.

This is an excellent option when you have a piece of soil that is containing lots of clay, or is in dire need of a boost in nutritional value.

If you're not able to create your own compost, you'll have to look for some commercial mixes that can be combined.

Commercial compost isn't ideal however, if there is the option of using it, it's better than none.

2. Peat Moss

Peat moss is a completely natural and is made up of plant material which has been decomposed, and then compressed over the course of millions of years. The more deeply peat moss gets buried and the more seasoned it gets.

Farmers frequently employ it to improve soil quality since it assists in loosening the soil, gives it a smoother texture, and assists in the retention of water.

Peat moss is regarded as an inedible resource due to the fact that it is so slow to develop and grow, therefore there are people who oppose its use in total. The benefit of a sq ft garden is the fact that it consumes the least amount of soil total. You increase the quality of the soil you're using but not all the soil that is in the garden. Furthermore the peat moss just added to the initial soil mix. Feeding to the soil later on is accomplished through the addition of compost.

3. Vermiculite

The last substance is known as vermiculite. It is Mica which has been extracted, crushed and heated until it literally explodes. The reason why it is so beneficial to this blend is because it is filled with air pockets. The vermiculite has tiny holes. This assists in loosening the soil, and also retain water.

Mixing All of It Together

The right amount of plants will require an amount of math. I suggest purchasing more than you'll require - the surplus can be stored to use later on or incorporated into the garden.

Vermiculite and peat-moss can produce a lot of dust in dry conditions, so it is recommended to use a mask while mixing the two. Avoid mixing them during the day that is windy.

The most efficient method of mixing the ingredients is to use the wheelbarrow. You could also employ a tarp. However, I have found that a wheelbarrow is easier to move the mixed soil, and then put it in the frame.

Mix all three ingredients in a way that you not discern any difference , and then lightly rinse the mix to ensure that it's just damp and not as smoky.

Place it in the frame in a loose manner, soaking it as you proceed. Don't over-pack the soil and make sure it's level to the edge of your frame. keep it there. It will settle after some time.

Planting

Now, it's time to start planting your squares. It will require some change of mind on your part since you're probably used to the traditional belief that vegetables require a lot of space.

Each square will be home to each one of the crops and the quantity of plants per square will be contingent on the dimensions of the plants.

Which plants should you choose?

Pick plants that fit the climate and location of your home. It is possible to consult your local nurseryman for specific guidance, but begin with the vegetables the family and you usually consume. You may test a couple of different things if you are interested however, you should make sure that the bulk of your produce will be ones you already know about.

The most important thing is ensuring the right spacing in the planting of your crop.

In general, you can categorize plants into four distinct groups:

* Small, like carrots, radishes and onions sixteen plants in a square

* Medium - similar to spinach, bush beans, and beets 9 plant species per square

Large - similar to the lettuce Swiss marigolds and even chard Four plants per square

Extra-large - like peppers, cabbages and broccoli - One plant for each square

When it comes to Swiss lettuce and chard, it could appear as if both plants grow too closely. The lettuce you are using is the "pick and serve" type of lettuce such as the Cos lettuce, and not one that has heads, as with Iceberg lettuce.

What happens is that you'll choose the leaves that are closest to you in the course of. The leaves should be bent from the base and not cut as this encourages the growth in new leaf growth. If you follow this procedure and picking the leaves that are on the outside it will leave plenty of room for each species of plant and a large crop, too.

What is the best place to plant each kind of Plant

The above diagram gives the idea for what crops you could plant in each square however, it's not a complete list. It is possible to plant different things in each square , or select lines of identical crop. You plant the quantity you'll need.

However, it's recommended to draw plans similar to the one below for your garden, indicating exactly what you will end in planting. Save it as a reference to use for the next season - it is not advisable to plant the same plant in the same location for two years in a row.

This increases the likelihood of a disease or pest that are present in the soil can negatively impact the crop next year.

Staggering Your Planting

It's also a great option to space your planting. When you grow six different lettuces simultaneously it is likely that you'll end up with a lot of lettuce that will be maturing at the exact time.

It is better to plant them at two week intervals throughout the growing season to ensure you can be sure of more consistent supply.

Be aware of the positioning in the bed

When it comes to deciding the best position for the bed, you should consider placing plants that require more attention in the rows to the left in order to make it easier for them to access. It's also sensible to plant higher-growing plants in the back or middle rows. Just make sure you have the ability to access every plant.

For instance, let's say that you plant corn. When you place it the front of your bush beans, you'll be unhappy because the beans mature ahead of the corn as well as the corn grows higher that the bean. Be guided by common sense when you're deciding which area to plant your plants.

If you have the space, you can grow an entire bed of one plant. This is particularly useful for those who want to cultivate vegetables for a crowd of people.

Companion Planting

Do not simply limit yourself to growing vegetables. Plants that are companions can improve the taste and health of plants. For example, chamomile can aid plants that are suffering recover quickly, while basil enhances the taste of tomatoes growing near.

Marigolds and pansies can assist to deter pests. Nasturtiums are an excellent trap crop that can draw bugs away from your garden.

Borage is a great plant to grow the event that you live in a hot climate. The plant is a refrigerant plant, which means that it can cool the soil surrounding it. This, in addition to its ability to gives some shade, make it a great choice for your vegetable gardens. Leaves can also be used to make a compost rich.

Companion plantation can be helpful in many other ways. For instance, the Native American Indians had what they called the three sisters. The three sisters would grow corn and later runner beans. When the crop grew it served as the beans with a framework to grow. Third sister, the pumpkin. The pumpkin was a cover for the ground, and also provided shades for the roots of two other sisters.

Planting for different seasons

Note the arrangement of the plants you plant for the first time to ensure that in the following seasons you must ensure that you don't plant the same crop in the same area. This is not a good idea since it could lead to soil diseases as well as a shortage in terms of nutrients.

When you practice the practice of rotation in your crops, you will ensure that your soil can regenerate between various varieties of crops. Certain crops can also help to make soils more nutritious for other crops. Beans, for instance help to fix nitrogen in the soil. This makes the soil perfect to plant cabbages in the coming season.

The most important thing is to conduct a bit of study into the most suitable time of the year when you can plant the crops. Broccoli is a good example. It is a fan of cooler temperatures and can quickly turn to seeds in hot temperatures. If you plant it too late in the season will result in florets that are not properly formed and generally will be an absolute waste of time.

Other plants, like beans, for instance are frost-resistant and can be harmed in colder climates. You can offer some protection to your plants using covers for frost, but plants that are frost-sensitive usually needs warmer temperatures in order to thrive in the first place.

It is important to experiment at home. Every garden has its own individual micro-climate. Therefore it's a good idea to record the plants you have put in as well as the date you planted it and the quality of the crop was.

If you keep good records You can stay current on the best choices for your particular area. Perhaps your yard is so it is protected that you don't or never, have frost. It might be warmer than the majority of areas in the vicinity. It could be that it isn't.

The primary thing to consider is that development slows during the winter months, as the soil is more frigid. Plants are less likely grow and are more likely to be hit by frost, therefore it is generally better to take winter into consideration in the growing season.

The land being left to lie in a state of slumber through winter isn't likely cause any harm in the end. It will aid in preventing the loss of essential nutrients from the soil.

If you're eager to get your garden going like most people are after the long winter, you can begin to grow seedlings in the cold of a frame or the warmer area. Seedlings are able to be raised and planted when the weather gets warmer and the chance of frost are gone.

How to Plant

When it comes to plant the vegetables, space is probably the most crucial factor, no matter if you're planting a garden of 16 carrots or one cabbage.

The space has been divided into equal squares. You can now split every square in equal pieces according to the number of plants you plan to put into it. For instance, if you plant lettuce seeds, then you'll divide the area into four equal portions. If you're planting carrots, then you'll split each of the sections into equal parts and so on.

Utilizing your fingers or a dibber, create holes in the center of each square. Make it large enough to completely cover the seeds as per the directions in the package.

Place a single seed in each hole, then cover them with dirt. Make sure to water it thoroughly.

If you opt to plant seedlings instead of seeds, the procedure is similar, except that you need to be able to squeeze the root ball in the space. Fill the hole after the seedling is placed and compact the soil until the seedling is secured.

Form a saucer-shaped shape around the seedling, so that water flows into it. Make sure to water the plant well using an easy spray. Also, make certain that your soil remains watered.

The process of transplanting can be an experience for the seedlings, so ensure they have the best chance of survival by digging the proper hole and providing them with ample water.

Maintenance of beds

The primary benefit of having elevated beds is the fact that they're much easier to keep. When you lay the weed cloth, or cardboard or newspaper right from the beginning and you'll be able to cut off many potential weeds in the first place.

If you're cautious about selecting the best sources of composting, a non-weedy one, you shouldn't face any issues with the weeds.

In reality, you'll likely only have to weed at least once per month or so. It really is that easy. All weeds that pop up are likely to be easily identified since they're unlikely to develop in the correct spot. Eliminating them completely is easy due to the texture of the soil.

Apart from weeding, you must ensure that your plants receive adequate water. Because these beds are smaller than normal gardens, they'll dry out faster. Be aware of signs that these beds have begun to dry out. Try to water them more frequently to ensure you are in the best position the excess water will evaporate therefore there is no need to be concerned about flooding your plants.

Just a small amount of water is required - one cup for each square will be sufficient. It is better to water your plants in the soil rather instead of letting the leaves get wet whenever it is possible. If you water the leaves you increase the chance of your plants getting Blight and mildew. By watering only the roots you let the plant receive the water exactly where it is the most required.

Make sure to leave a bucket of water close to the garden so that it can be heated with the sunlight. You don't enjoy the shock of a cold shower don't you? And neither do your plants.

An irrigation drip system offers an easy maintenance alternative that can be easily and cheaply installed. The image below illustrates the professional model, but it's easy to replicate at home with minimal expense.

All you require is:
• A faucet accessory to the hose
* A few long hosepipes
* Y-connectors are used for the hose
* Three-point connector to the hose
* Knife
* Hose stakes to be secured

Set the bucket in a raised location and it must be above the beds, so that gravity pulls off the water. It is necessary to build funnels on the ground adjacent every plant.

Place a length of hosepipe into the funnel adjacent to each plant. It should be similar to this.

Connect the hoses of each length to the connectors. Then use the three-point connector to connect the two main hoses. Attach the bucket's faucet and secure the hoses to ensure that they are flat.

Attach a last length of the hose with the connector, and the faucet. (If there's no faucet in the vicinity you can attach it to the bucket using an attachment to the faucet.)

It'll look similar to it does.

Then, make holes into the pipe close to each plant. (The water hose that connects the faucet won't be able to make holes). If you wish to get water it, all you have to do is switch to turn on your faucet. The water will fill the hose and then flow across the pipes, providing an exact amount of water. It is more efficient than a sprinkler system , and more efficient when the possibility of evaporation is an issue due to the more extreme temperatures.

Mulching

If temperatures are excessive, then you could aid to safeguard your seedlings by spreading a mulch of dead or straw. It serves two functions as it prevents the soil from drying out and helps it hold in water and reduces the development of weeds too.

Straw is readily available however, you could also think about using grass clippings. Ideally, they are supposed to be drying before being sprayed on the plants.

If you can locate this, Eucalyptus mulch can be beneficial in keeping bugs and pests and protecting to the soil.

Wood chips are also beneficial, but they should not be used in the event of a problem with insects on your property.

Pruning and pinching

Some plants may benefit from pinching or trimming from time to the time. Pruning the crown leaves will promote the growth of lateral branches in plants like bush beans . Also, vines need to be pruned once and again to prevent the growth that is excessive. While it may seem counterintuitive to trim the edges of vines, or to remove flowers that are overgrown however, it makes sense because you're helping the plant conserve its energy. The energy employed by the plant in creating the additional foliage can be channeled into the growth of fruit which will allow to increase the yield in time.

Instead of buying 10 small pumpkins You can choose several large and delicious ones that will mature to maturity.

Monitoring for Disease And Pests

It will also be important to examine the plants regularly from time time to check whether or not they've got problems or diseases. The plants are more resistant to diseases and pests due to the robust mix of growing materials However, it is important to be on guard.

If you discover insects or diseases, try to eliminate the problem as fast as you can. Making a simple spray with garlic along with water and a small amount of dishwashing detergent will go a long way to keep your plants free of pests.

Apply the mixture to leaves, and repeat the process after it's rained or you've rinsed it off using water.

Snails can be a real nuisance that can do many damages within a short amount of time.

Remove pests manually whenever you are able and create barriers to stop them, if you can. For instance, snails can be sprayed with finely crushed eggshells, vermiculite , or sharp gravel on the plants. Their soft bodies are unable to endure the hardness. You can keep them away from plants completely by placing the netting of vegetables over them, as this blogger.

If you decide to go on a snail hunt Take a bucket that has plenty of salt. put them in the bucket. The salt will cause them to dehydrate and eliminate them. It may sound a bit unpleasant and after you've been the victim of a devastating crop caused by snails, you'll not feel nearly as bad.

With the square-foot garden but the chickens are much more likely be a nuisance and you can guard your garden easily by building a bird cage made of chicken wire put in support for chicken wire in the four edges of your square. Then fix it to the bed's frame with one side which can be removed to allow you to be able to access the bed.

For bigger pests such as deer, all you need is change to a stronger wire and provide support.

You might require replenishing the soil every now and then to help the plants through their blooming time, however it won't be frequently as it is in your regular garden. Just dig in some compost every year to replenish your soil.

Be sure to monitor the soil throughout the rest season, and especially when you have high-feeders like cabbage. If the soil is cracked despite having plenty of water this is a sign that it is in need of more compost.

Chapter 6: Harvesting The Fruits Of Your Work

Now is the time to move on to the best part, actually picking your herbs and vegetables.

Harvesting

In these smaller gardens you can harvest whenever the vegetables are in season. By constantly snipping off the leaves that surround the lettuce as well as Swiss chard, you will make sure that the plant lives for a longer time - cutting it helps it expand more quickly, as long as you continue taking only the outer leaves. The plant will eventually grow into seed, but before that, you'll receive a large amount of fruit.

When it comes to plants like beans, picking them typically encourages beans to produce more, and so frequent harvesting is advised.

When you are harvesting your fruit or vegetables, pull off the plant with care to not damage the plant. Let the fruits and vegetables to develop on the vines for an amazing taste.

A garden that is planted near the home will help you take more vegetables as well as herbs, which will help you to eat healthier and prepare more delicious meals.

Allow Some Plants to Seed

If you'd want to, you can allow some or two plants like a lettuceplant, to grow into seed, and then harvest seeds to save them for the next season. This will help lower the cost of replenishing your garden over the coming years.

When you harvest the fruit or seeds for seeds, let them sit to dry for a few weeks to ensure they'll be able to last until next year.

The seeds should be stored in envelopes or bags of paper in a dry and well-ventilated cabinet. On the bag's front note on the bag the names of your plants as well as the year that you harvested it.

In general, the seeds will last for about a year However, it's probably better to keep the seeds for a single year. You can plant what you require as well as a few more to be safe. Then donate the seeds you've got instead of keeping the entire crop.

It is possible to exchange with other people who are interested and you can try different kinds of ice cream.

Making beds ready to plant again

By planting square foot you can expect your plants to mature in different stages which makes replanting less work. It is possible to harvest 3 crops in a square growing season. You really don't have to take much time to prepare your beds for the next season's crop.

All you have to do is harvest the crop, remove the plant, if necessary, and then plant the next crop. It is best than to not plant the exact same thing twice in the row, if that is possible.

If you'd like choose to, you could consider refilling your soil with green manure. It's an excellent way to add more nutrients naturally . It's basically similar to allowing soil to be left to recover from the growing of vegetables.

Green Manure

The green crops of clover, mustard, fenugreek and alfalfa can be very nutritious for the soil. Plant them when you've harvested the last crop or toward the end of winter.

When they reach approximately a foot high Cut them down, and then either add them directly into the soil or add them to your compost pile.

If you mix them into the soil, you'll have to wait for at about two weeks before planting new crops in order to let the process of decomposition be established. Plants that are decomposing can cause fire to seeds, which is why it's ideal to avoid this breathing time.

Other occasions to think about green Manure

Alfalfa is a tree with a vast root system which can assist in breaking the clayey soil. You should think about plant it in the location that you're experiencing this issue in. You can leave it for one year or so, before digging it out. The root system can help to break down the clay, and when it is decomposing, it will provide lots of nutrients.

Yarrow is not classified as a green manure, however it can be extremely beneficial for improving soil conditions. Simply plant it and let it for one year or two years. If the Yarrow begins to take over, you will know that the soil has been better. You can cut off the Yarrow back and then dig it into the same way as any other soil improvement product.

They can also be utilized to improve the quality of your compost significantly. Comfrey is a herb that is particularly nutritious for plants and assists in activating compost.

Chapter 7: The Way To Acquire Space For Farming Space

Although it might seem insignificant to mention it however, it should be mentioned at least once, and that is to respect the "Do start with a small" rule. In the end, with a backyard mini-farm there is no need to have much space. Another thing to note; if you are planning to keep any animals pick the smaller ones.

How do you create the elusive farm space?

Container Gardening

In areas where space for farming is severely restricted, only a handful of options can compete with container gardening. The majority of crops are able not just to expand but also to thrive in containers. In addition, a large portion of those plants will also do well inside. The most important thing to know about containers is the fact that they tend to dry out very quickly. Regular, constant watering is vital for achieving great yields. For trees that are grown in containers they require some form of protection must be provided for the trees. This is due to the fact that their roots aren't so well-insulated like those of trees that grow outside.

Raised Beds

They are an excellent option for gardening in the backyard with regards to space. The thing that makes them stand out as an option, is the fact that their yield is always greater when compared to other methods of farming. For square-foot gardening it is a grid of 1 foot squares is laid on the ground to help the planter to grow more extensively.

Intercropping

Intercropping is when you can do is plant slow-growing and fast-growing crops in a single. This is basically the meaning behind intercropping, and it's a life time saver when it comes down to making the most of space. The thing that every backyard mini-farm proprietor must be aware of is that the majority of the plants that consume a lot of space will not utilize the space until they've reached maturation. You can make the most of this fact by throwing some radishes that grow quickly as well as some salad leaves or even beets in your soil in between rows of your larger plants. At the point that your plants have reached maturity and require all the space available the radishes and other crops will are gone.

Vertical Gardening

Vertical gardening is the urban agriculture's latest craze. If you plant your vegetables that are vining to rise upwards, what you're doing is reducing the amount of space you are using for the soil. This will boost your overall yield for each square foot, since it's much more feasible to accommodate more plants in the space in your garden. The ability to save space isn't the only reason you should think about vertical gardening. Before you start this new innovative gardening technique it is important to keep in mind the following points:

To prevent shade from different plants, put trellises along the Northern edge.

Make sure you anchor your trellises. This will protect against heavy rains and winds. It is recommended to be able to anchor them to an average minimum of 24 inches in depth.

How can you increase your vertical growth?

Tomatoes

It is possible to trellis non-bush varieties or indeterminate ones. They will continue to grow, and produce fruits up to when frost is present.

Peas & Cucumbers

Choose non-bush plants for vertical gardening. The varieties with bush will require no trellising since their vines only extend up to 6 feet long.

Gourds, Pole beans, and Melons

There is an unwritten rule in relation to trellising. Any plant with fruit that is smaller than a volley ball may be Trellised. In the end the vines will contain enough steel to support the fruits and hammocks to hold them up is not necessary.

Pumpkins and squash

Small-fruited pumpkins and the non-bush varieties such as miniature pumpkins, the buttercup and acorn squash are all suitable for gardening vertically.

What can you grow?

Even if you're able to grow your plants in small areas, you'll still would like to have a substantial number of plants. If you don't you might be able to be able to eliminate "thriving" in the gardening vocabulary. Your plants will need to supply you with plenty of food items that look and taste great. Some plants stand out as perfect for small-scale backyard farms. Let's an examination of a few.

Basil

The majority of gardeners opt for basil. It's not a coincidence that this happens. The delicate basil leaves stimulate your senses and add fresh taste to pesto, salad dressings, and so on. There are more than 80 varieties of basil along with a variety of miniature varieties available that are suitable to mini farms. Pistou is the tiniest one, and is perfect for window boxing.

Basil is incredibly easy to cultivate and can be purchased from many seed catalogs.

Chard

The "cut-and-re-grow" varieties of plants are a farmer's most-loved. With Chard cutting the leaves triggers an increase in the number them. This phenomenon, when combined along with the straight style and its vibrantly colored appearance makes it the ideal gardening plant for your backyard garden. Rainbow Chard also works well in tight spaces.

Since Chard is an beet-related plant It is quite simple to cultivate it from seeds. To ensure proper spacing, the seedlings must undergo some degree of thinning. If the containers you have are small, you can start with transplants - there is no need for thinning in these.

Eggplant

The variety known as the oriental eggplant is well-known because of its compact shape, which makes it a perfect choice for spaces-based farmers. They are so amazing in their growth that picking one of the varieties that you like best leaves one in a bind. Some knowledgeable individuals have stated that it is the Ping Tung Long variety earns the top spot on their lists. This bias is based on looks only, and not necessarily because they are smaller in shape compared to other varieties. Because the plant is small and also compact, it is perfect to cub. The flavor is mildly delicious and popular with a lot of people.

For the best results, plant your seeds indoors, and in warmer weather transfer the seeds to pots or planters.

Tips: At the beginning, you should include your use of the bottom heating. This makes the process of germination much easier and more certain. The best place to place your seedling tray is on a germinating mat and set it at around 80 degrees F. The fridge's top can also be used, since the seeds will stay warm thanks to the heat created through the appliances.

Hot Peppers

It is difficult to identify a plant which is as suitable for mini-farms in the backyard as spicy peppers do. For example, Black Hungarian pepper is so vibrant and vibrant that keeping it in the garden is an offence in gardening. It's best to place it on the patio in pots of small size can also enhance the appearance of your patio. When the pepper is growing in size, the fruit will initially be green before turning black, and once it is ripe it will change to a vibrant red hue. The plants can reach a height of 30 to 36 inches, which makes the plants a bit big to fit into an ordinary window. However, larger pots are not a problem. Start seeds indoors and transfer them to pots, and planters during the warmer months.

Tomato

Fast in their growth and abundant in fruit tomatoes can overwhelm the trellises with a force that can be overwhelming in the process. However, several tests have helped growers come up with varieties that are smaller that can be grown in smaller areas. For instance, Cherry Cascade variety grows sturdy in the hanging basket, and can produce tons of tomatoes.

The fruit of the Cherry Cascade tomato plants can vary from the tiny size of a marble for kids all the way to a golf ball. It is deliciously tomato-flavored in contrast to the sweet flavor that is found in many cherry tomatoes. They are extremely resistant to drought, and what are more important, they are resistant to cracking and the ailment known as rot, which often infests many varieties of tomatoes.

Mesclun

The word mesclun literally means various greens. This is believed to be due to the wild weeds hunted by the poor in Europe as a supplement to their strained and limited diets.

The varieties available of today, including Arugula and mustards that are quick-growing, aren't ideal for growing in containers. However, it is possible to make your own mesclun that is container-friendly. It is possible to think about Italian endives, as well as Escaroles. They are easy to harvest in leaf-by-leaf. Another thing to be aware of: spring companies provide mixesthat are that are suitable for the specific type of season that you are in. Start with a mix for spring. After harvesting, plant another mesclun mix which is robust enough to stand up to the summer heat. You can then you can follow that with a 3rd plant of autumn greens. Some examples are cold-tolerant kales as well as collard.

Lettuce

It's a hit, and is available in all kinds of size and color. There's a thing you might not be aware of: the best results come from mixing it in your backyard mini-farm. It is important to grow a variety of lettuce inside your containers, or in your planting space.

Lettuce doesn't take very long to grow to the maturity stage. It can grow from seeds to salad in about 45-days (about one and one half months). If you'd like to spread through the growing season (which is a wise choice) take them down leaf by leaf, or store an additional crop, whose purpose will be to fill the space left after harvesting your lettuce.

Edible Flowers

This is a must-have for the majority of mini farms owners since the charm and beauty they bring to your garden is about unbeatable. The best choices are

Nasturtiums and viola varieties and the ever-popular calendula. What sets them apart is that, even after they've been picked, they've got the ability to continue growing all through the summer.

If it turns out to be difficult to locate transplants, the majority of edible flowers are sold in seeds anyway. The process is straightforward: just push the seeds into the soil in which you would like the plants to grow and the job is done.

Pole Beans

It's usually feasible in the event that vertical garden is used. The well-known Italian family heirloom "Trionfo Violetto" is a favorite among many. It's distinguished by its lush green appearance as well as a stunning purple underneath. When midsummer arrives, a row of lavender flowers makes their appearance. They are followed by beans that have purple pods.

How do I start? What are the essential requirements to each one of the above?

Basil

If you plant plants in pots, make sure to use big pots. This will reduce the risk of drying out after the summer heat arrives. A water-retaining polymer can be useful- not only will it help ensure that the soil is perfectly moist, but it will also cut down on the amount of interval between watering, which will save you the time as well as effort. Following the last frost of spring, allow two weeks before setting out your plants. Planting them in the summer is a good idea as well. One rule to be aware of is to place your plants at minimum 12 inches apart. They are very sensitive to frost So be sure to ensure that your plants are protected during an extended cold snap. Basil typically thrives in rich and moist, but well-drained soils. A pH between 6 and 7 is the ideal pH.

Chard

Chard thrives in moist, fertile soils that have a pH of 6 to 6.8. Make sure you space your plants at minimum 12 inches apart. Prior to planting, incorporate fertile amendments that are nitrogen-rich into your soil. Compost is a huge help also.

As with all vegetables, chard is a good choice when the watering is regular. If the rainfall is not plentiful, you can make sure to water the chard at least 1.5 inches every week. Be sure to keep your watering steady and consistent. Use organic mulch (there are a myriad of mulches you can make use of to accomplish such a purpose) in order to ensure that the soil stays cool and humid and to reduce the amount of weeds. Mulching is also a fantastic method to keep your plant's leaves in good condition, thus reducing the risk of developing plant diseases that can affect your leaves.

Eggplant

These gorgeous, elegant plants thrive and are stunning in containers, the most decorative borders, raised beds and the classic in-ground garden.

The eggplant is addicted to warmth and thrives best in areas that are well-drained. To get the best results, go to beds raised and enhanced by manure that has been composted. But any soil with a pH range between 6 to 6.3 can be used for growing eggplant. Because eggplant needs warm soil for its growth, when grown in cool climates It is best if you plant them in large dark-colored pots or containers.

For the most effective fertilization of your soil, fertilize it with a properly balanced timed release, or even organic fertilizer. Be sure to adhere to the guidelines on the label of the container. In addition it is recommended to mix in approximately 2-inches of composted manure in order to assist in the retention of water and fertilizer in the soil.

Hot Peppers

Peppers are excellent because they thrive in well-drained, sunny spaces , as well as dark containers. They can thrive in almost every environment. Since peppers grow in a straight shape, stalking will benefit tremendously. This will stop the breakage of branches that are brittle particularly when the fruiting season arrives.

To grow properly peppers are thriving in soils that have pH levels ranging from 6.06 to 6.7. However, this doesn't mean this is the only pH threshold: slightly acidic conditions around 7.5 are not harmful to plants. Mix 3 - to 5-inch thick layer organic compost in each planting hole. Organic matter can help keep the soil moist, and it is crucial for pepper to flourish. After planting the pepper, you should mulch each plant to keep the soil cool and also humid.

In the 6 weeks after planting (as soon when the peppers begin to bloom and produce fruit) Just remove your mulch and sprinkle some fertilizer on the base of each plants, then cover the mulch prior to watering. This will aid in maintaining the plant's strength during the duration of its growth.

Tomato

To get the best flavor, tomatoes require around eight hours in exposure sun every day. This means that you'll have to keep your plants away from their feet (staking or trellising is a way to achieve this). The best thing to do is to choose an appropriate plan of support prior to plant, and then after you have planted begin adding the support immediately.

To ensure the highest growth tomatoes require the pH of their soil to be between 6.8 to 6.8. It is important to be aware that they require quite the variety of nutrients to ensure nutrition. Make sure you add 3-4 inches of manure from compost in your garden. The compost is essential for the growth of your plants, because it stores the nutrients and moisture in the soil it is time the plant is mature enough to make use of it.

Be sure to mulch the soil with approximately 3 inches worth of soil. This will help keep the weeds down and will also help to increase the presence of moisture within the soil. To get the most effective tomato mulch there are few alternatives to straw and shredded leaves. If your region is susceptible to droughts in summer what you should do is to use soaker hosesor drip irrigation or any other method to ensure an even moisture level in the soil. This will prevent cracking and the rot of the end of the flower at the horizon.

Lettuce

While lettuce is extremely successful in hot , sunny conditions however, it is one of those plants that actually thrive in shade. Lettuce is also amazing because you can cultivate plenty of it in one pot that is big enough.

For best results, look for soils that are rich, moist and brimming with organic matter. Maintain the pH at 6 to 7.0 to achieve the best outcomes. Fertilize, and then lime according to test guidelines.

Lettuce thrives best at temperatures that range between 45 and 80 degrees Celsius. It is not recommended to grow it in hot weather as it can make it bitter and unappealing, and colder weather is only able to keep it frozen. When it is well-rooted There are bibb varieties like the Buttercrunch which can withstand an adequate amount of frost.

Pole Beans

It doesn't matter whether you have been gardening for a while or you're making your first foray into gardening, pole beans must be on your list of things to be done. Pole beans aren't only durable and easy to maintain, but they also boast some of the best and abundant produce of all vegetables. They also age quickly and to top it all off, almost everyone enjoys snap beans. Even the youngest children have the taste of these.

Snap beans are simple to cultivate in all well-drained, fertile soils. Warmth must be a an element of the growing equation throughout the year. You should wait until your last frost arrived and gone before proceeding to plant your seeds. If you are spacing your plants, make sure to leave minimum 8 inches in between every plant. If you have a double-row, where two rows are planted with 12 inches between rows, will yield largest amount of beans per square foot. For a consistent good harvest, plan up another row of plants three to four weeks after you have planted your first set.

In conjunction with the bacteria within the soil beans produce nitrogen, the most essential nutrient needed to grow the beans.

Keep the pole beans well-weeded and mulch them over the areas between the plants to keep their water and also to prevent persistent problems caused by the weeds. Furthermore, mulch can help keep the pods of pole beans clean as well as a great convenience in the case of snap beans.

Soil Preparation

All vegetables require a healthy soil to grow. If the soil is dry and dry, the food that your plants produce will reflect the low quality of the soil that you are working with. Soft, rich soils that have abundant nutrients allow the root system to penetrate deep into the soil and soak up vital nutrients that are needed to produce healthy plants. Here are some helpful tips that can be very beneficial when you are preparing your soil.

Clean the area

This is the simplest step. Take the pebbles and rocks all around the area.

The soil should be loosen

With a power tiller or a garden fork, you can work the soil until it reaches 8 inches of depth. 12 inches is more beneficial in order to protect your garden.

Enhance the soil

Utilizing a tiller or fork, which is the one closest to the soil, apply compost manure or soil conditioner to the soil. In addition to being essential in supplying nutrients to soil and increasing its capacity to hold water it also aids in drainage and stimulating beneficial microorganisms activities. It is also possible to include sulfur or lime to control the soil's pH according to the requirements. Utilizing the garden rake (a fork works perfectly if you don't aren't using a the rake) then level then smooth out the dirt until it's even.

If the soil is a bit difficult, you may want to think about raised beds. Simply put the soil that is good over the rest in the dirt. The more deep your beds are the better. If raised beds are not an the best option, you can plant your plants in pots. They'll be just as well.

The great thing about soil is the fact that it continues to improve throughout the seasons through the consistent application of compost and manure. As time passes the soil will begin to resemble what farmers call black gold, a very dense, dark-colored soil that is rich in nutrients. Yet, it drains exceptionally well.

It is essential to recognize how the earth is full of livingmicroorganisms which are responsible for the general fertility of the soil.

Containers for gardening and pots What size are they? What materials are they made from?

There is the option of selecting clay pots that could be glazed, or they might not be plastic pots, no matter how beautiful or ugly or even wooden pots regardless of size or small. This is only the beginning of the list however. There are a few things to think about when you contemplate gardening in containers:

Size

In most cases larger pots (in regards to both dimensions and width) are perceived to be more attractive. This is especially true when you have larger-sized plants, like for example tomatoes. If your pots are large and large, the possibility of your plants being squeezed is much less than when you use smaller pots.

A half-cut whiskey or wine barrel is a big and inexpensive container that can hold a variety of different vegetables. It can, for instance, hold 10 lettuce heads, around 10 bush-bean plants, around two tiny tomato plants and even four or five tiny cucumber varieties. If you're in need of any of them, a visit to the garden center or nursery can get you one in a matter of minutes.

Material

The materials a container is constructed of could affect the amount of times it needs to be refilled and also how long the pot lasts. Pots made from dry substances (an instance being clay pots) are more likely to dry out than plastic and wood counterparts, meaning you'll have to water them more often. This is particularly true for areas that are windy or dry.

The essential features to have for your containers for the garden

Here are a few key aspects that you can't afford to ignore:

Drainage

Each pot you choose to plant will need drainage holes to be drilled in. The best part is that most of them have drainage holes. But, wooden barrels do not come with these (they are designed to keep the remnants of wine out, remember) So you'll need to do some work and drill holes yourself. Around 10 holes of 1-inch diameters, should suffice.

A saucer to place under the pot.

The saucer basically holds the water that flows out of the holes, making sure that the dish does not become stained or stain anything it is sitting on.

Wheels (for old-fashioned mobility)

A majority of nurseries will offer pots that have wheels to facilitate mobility. Be certain to verify the wheels in the event of a problem.

Planting, Watering & Possible dangers
Potted Container Planting Instructions for Potted Containers

The first thing to be aware of when purchasing the plant is that it's had rough experiences on the journey the home of your choice. It is likely that the plants were transported by hot trucks and have been through rough hands in the process. So they could be in a kind of "shock" following the transport. But don't worry they can perk up fast.

The watering of your plants is likely to be the most important factor. Just water your plants when you recognize that your soil is drying up. In the event that extreme temperatures are the issue you must take the necessary steps to ensure your plants are provided with enough shade to flourish in.

Preparations for planting

Create a large hole to accommodate the transplants. For plants that are young be sure that your hole is very deep. The hole must be 5 inches deeper than where the roots of the plant go.

Planting your vegetable

Put some dirt in on the inside of the hole. The purpose of scooping the soil initially was to loosen it up for the plants to establish. Set your plant straight up and then make the soil fill in the space. If you'd like you could add the top soil in addition to other soil. After filling the hole, ensure to put in tiny amount of water. It will make sure that there are no air pockets are left within the dirt. It will also provide beneficial water for the plant.

The watering of your plant

The majority of plants you plant will require watering them often, especially during the initial few weeks. However, a humid atmosphere is not what your plants are searching for, so try not to overwater it. In fact the plants that are overwatered will look like an under-watered plant. If you find that your plants are taking on a an unnatural look, turn off with your watering and watch the changes that occur.

Mulch

It is often claimed mulch will be the garden's best allies. It will help to hold back the weeds and grasses that compete for nutrients with your flowering plants, while also aiding the soil in retaining water. It is important to select the mulch to be at least two inches thick to accommodate your vegetable garden.

Care and watering instructions

In hot weather, you should ensure that your vegetable gardens are watered at least three or four times during the week. The process of watering is vital one, and shouldn't be ignored. The water must be directed downwards, in order that the roots don't get attracted to the surface of the soil, which could cause much more damage. The best way to go about this is to set an empty cup into the soil of your garden. Continue to water it, and continue to water until at the very least an inch of water has been collected within the cup. If you see water puddles across the top, proceed forward, but keep checking to see if the water is soaking into creating a soil that is damp in the way it is supposed to.

Be aware of your garden to find "indicator" plant species. The indicator plant will usually be the first plant to die in the mini-farm that is located in the backyard. If you notice the plant with its droopy foliage when you notice them, you'll realize that it's time to give your plants a good watering. Most often, squashes, watermelon and cucumbers make the ideal indicator plants because broad leaves are able to handle an increased demand for water. However, of course the ideal scenario is one where the plant is drooping because of your constant irrigation, but gardening isn't always perfect.

Make every effort to ensure that water stays within the soil. A basic mulch (straw or pine needles make great examples) will fit perfectly between the soil with the solar rays. A mulch that is two of inches will make a an enormous difference with the event of summer heat and will serve the purpose of a shade or cloth shade that shields the soil from sun's direct rays that could lead to the drying out of water. This water could be what your plant needs to thrive and grow.

Possible dangers

If you are able to discern and recognize the symptoms of blight , or even wilt that can put you in a better position to combat the illness. These are the two most prevalent diseases and the best way to manage these.

Blights

Blights are characterized by the leaves of plants drooping in the wind, withering, and eventually dying. In the future, different plant parts may begin to turn brown.

Blights includes fire blight blight of alternaria (also an early form of blight) phytophthora Blight (commonly called late blight) and bacterial blight.

In order to prevent the spread of the blights, it is recommended to take down the plants infected and eliminate all the plant waste.

Cankers

They usually develop on stems that are woody. They can be in the form of sunken areas, cracks or raised areas of dead or abnormal plant tissue. At times, they could be visible and release their fluids. They can harm the plant as they can cause shoots to girdle, causing all the above to wilt and then die.

Examples include Cytospora canker as well as Nectria canker.

The best way to manage cankers is to restrict the cutting of branches and also removing any branches that are diseased.

Harvesting: When, when to harvest, what to harvest and storage for harvest

This is the truth: timing is the sole factor that determines the proper harvesting timings. When you master the art of timing, it's simple to have an unbeatable yield. There are hints to help you harvest the aspect of the farming. Learn more about the subject to become educated.

When you harvest, you are able to develop a better understanding of your vision. This is how it works: with time, you will be able to tell from the appearance of the produce, whether the plants are ready to harvest or not. Most of the times, this happens after a couple of years or as.

For instance, pumpkins can appear large enough for cutting and taken and consumed. But, it's best to wait to harvest until the stems are dry. The pumpkin becomes tough and then the vine dying. If you harvest the pumpkin earlier than this the seeds could be unripe and, even more importantly the flavor might not have reached its peak. The stalks should be cut to a length at least 5 centimeters away from the fruit of the pumpkin in order to prolong the shelf time. Pumpkins should be left to dry (preferably in the sunlight) for several days , so that the skin is not brittle.

Usually, the time of harvesting will be determined by two elements:

The varieties being cultivated

Weather conditions

In the instance of beans you can choose to pick them while they are still tender and young or hold off until they are fully mature. When they've reached maturity it is imperative to pick and picked since it is during this that they're at their most nutritious. Zucchinis are typically harvested when they're young (will measure around 10 centimeters in length, if the goal for them to be picked) because they can increase in size at a rapid rate and can turn into mushy bone marrow within a few hours.

Keep in mind that when you are picking leafy vegetables generally, it is recommended to pick them in late afternoon so that you don't get the benefit of excessive nitrates. When you pick them, the afternoon can allow the sun to transform those nitrogen compounds that are within the plants.

How do I Harvest

If handled rough plants can get damaged. It is best to have a sharp knife and a pair or scissors too. The basket is ideal to keep the salad leaves fresh from bruising as well as unnecessary dirt

There are a few vegetables that you can cutwhile harvesting:

Beans - This is especially true to bush beans. Make sure you cut them and put them in your basket.

Beetroot - If feasible (nature can be a bit tricky, making it nearly impossible to do this at times) take off the leaves and make salads for your meals. Of course, you'll need to take out the roots at some point and when you are harvesting the leaves, ensure to keep a portion of the leaves to ensure that the plant will be capable of efficiently converting photosynthetic material.

Capsicum & Chillis - These can be cut when they are still green in colour, however if you're willing to be patient, you can be patient and wait until they are red or orange , or even yellow (this will depend on the kind of variety you're looking for). Be aware that stems tend to be very fragile (pulling away from them likely result in an unwelcome length of stem).

Lettuce is a popular choice for farmers. Many tend to cut off all leaves, leaving the plant in a bare state. It is best to cut off a few leaves, but leave the rest to ensure that the plant is capable of producing energy and create food. After a significant dose of seaweed foliar spray, small-sized leaves will sprout on the plant.

Herbs — We all have a few herbs that we've identified as our top picks. When it comes to herbs, the temptation to select them all from the plant is almost always evident, which can result in dried herbs when you're done with picking. It is best to grow different varieties of herbs to supplement the herb that you picked.

When harvesting your herb, make certain to cut off the tender and young leaves (you will require the leaves (the stems, not so as much)). Be sure to not remove more than half of the flowers on the plant or it will cease to produce. The harvesting of herbs like sage occurs in the morning, once the dew has evaporated off the leaves but, again prior to the sun's heat and rays disperse the vital oils which give sage its delicious taste and aroma. This time of year the herb will be in its prime.

Chapter 8: Beginning The Farm Small Farm

Small Farm

According to USDA Small farms is one that has a gross cash farm income of less than $250,000, whether commercial or not. Most of these types of farms are run by rural residents.

Farming is an activity which involves a variety of things from animal production to the cultivation of crops. There are many lucrative possibilities for those who want to begin their mini-farming venture either for fun or as an occupation.

They are classified as follows:

* Fish farming is the raising of fish

* Tree Nursery - Seed making new plants available for sale prior to their maturity

* Dual crop farming - cultivating multiple crops on the same area

* Dairy farming- the breeding of animals to produce milk

* Herb gardening- the growing of herbs

* Bee FarmingYou already know that Beekeepers create things like honey.

* Aquaponics - the farmers in this region produce both aquatic animals as well as crops grown in water(hydroponics)
* Microgreens farming - the growing of a specific kind of tiny vegetable
* Vegetable landscaping - investing hugely in growing vegetables
* Cannabis farming in an area where it is permitted, the growing of the plant is an alternative.
* Rooftop Tea GardenThis is very beneficial in areas with little land area
* Snail farming, raising this tiny creature to sell to consumers

There are also mushroom farms and Poultry farming. Flower farms, Animal Petting Farm, Fruit picking farms, etc.

At the start it is suggested to sketch and plan out the way you want your farm to look. You must make sure that you've answered these following questions:

1. Is farming the best thing to pursue at this time at this point in my career? Your answer is dependent on your motives such as farm-related knowledge, work, style

and your own personal sentiment or love for farming.

2. Have you established your goals? If you are considering this as a pastime or increase your income, it's a part-time work or you would like to turn it into part-time work.

3. Animals and crops that will likely be your primary goal, or both? If you own an area of half an acre, for instance, it could be used to maintain a small vegetable garden and laying hens. Therefore, you have to decide on the area for your own

4. What is your financial capability? It will affect the amount of your farm and what you are able to manage to afford.

5. Have you created a specific plan for your first year? This plan should address both how to handle your risk and benefits, as a newbie.

6. Have you devised an approach to monitoring? Farming demands a specific kind of monitoring and reassessment to be able to quickly alter your plans in the event of an emergencies.

A few of the most basic equipment for farmers will include
* Cutlass - used to cut branches from trees,
* Shovel - used for digging soil, etc.
* Spade-similar use to the shovel.
* Hoe- for tilling
* Bolo- to cut to weeds
* Wheelbarrowfor transporting material
* Rake- to remove dirt from the farm
* Hand Trowel - for transplanting seeds
Hand Fork-to mix organic matter with soil
* Secateurs- to trim flowers and leaves
* Shearsfor trimming of trees
* Axe- to cut tall stems
* Crowbar - for lifting stone from ground
* Watering Can - for irrigation of the crops
* Sprayers_ to spray insecticides
* Hammerfor driving nails into wood and etc.

Understanding and monitoring of Soil Health Methods
If you want to make it in the field of agriculture you must learn as any farmers, to be aware of the importance about soils,

chemicals and biological components which are essential for a well-groomed soil. Understanding and managing your soil can be a chance to succeed in this field.

Experts are in favor of an agricultural method that is environmentally friendly as a means to ensure the soil's high in which plants need to grow. proper growth.

Therefore, you must identify and follow the soil management method that does not just improve the quality of your crops , but also improves the soil.

As a resource that is considered to be extremely important Certain soil practices may enhance or decrease its value for agriculture.

Soil is a complex ecosystem, which includes living organisms, plant roots mineral particles, as well as organic matter. It also has an unusually controlled flow of water-air and nutrients.

Soil management includes every activity focused on improving the soil. It is important to put in place a an effective plan for recycling nutrients and pest control strategies, as well as water and air delivery to soil in order to reap the most benefits from the soil.

Nutrients Recycling

This is how nutrients, be they organic or mineral are introduced, removed and altered within the soil. Nutrients can be found in soil in the form of organic as well as inorganic minerals and when combined with water, form the solution for soil.

You must also be aware of the terms used in soil nutrients.

*Cation exchange websites Positively charged nutrients. Plants require enough Macronutrient cation such as calcium. Organic matter's negatively charged sites, store these plant nutrients with positive charges.

Organic matter organic matter: living and once-living substances which, through decomposition, provide soil nutrients.

* Decomposition is the process of breaking down the organic elements of soil into substances that benefit the soil. This is done by microorganisms

* Mineralization is the release of nutrients to soil after decomposition.

Why is it important to manage your soil properly? It's to provide it with the necessary amount of nutrition at an right moment, and also reduce the loss of nutrients to the surrounding environment. Organic matter is rich in nutrients, but they can only be useful to plants after it has been transformed into inorganic or minerals that are needed and can be easily absorbed through the decomposition process and mineralization of microorganisms.

You might also wish to know how this process takes place. It's called the soil food web

Soil Foodweb

This is to ensure that the activities of all living organisms in the soil, including minor organisms that are not visible as well as larger ones, aid in decomposition via a microbial process called mineralization.

Soil PH

It is the method to measure the activity of the hydrogen (H+) in the soil's solution. It regulates a variety of micronutrients and makes them (eg zinc, iron) more accessible as the pH becomes more acidic.

Biological Pest Organisms' Control

The soil organism ecosystem is vital for farmers because, through biological pest control - the recourse to natural predators of the organism to eliminate it, pests are reduced, which results in an agro-ecosystem that is healthy. For instance, beetles are the living enemies of soil to insects which is why they are essential in bio-based pest management.

Regulating Air and Water in the soil

As you've guessed, that plants require oxygen as well as water at their root for survival. Water is stored within the pores that surround soil particles and soil aggregates. The pores that exist between and within soil aggregates determines the flow of gases and water, as well as the amount of water that is retained.

Naturally, macropores with larger pores guarantee proper aeration as well as rapid infiltration of rainwater; however, the opposite is true for micropores since it holds more water. Both are necessary for a healthy soil

You need to know the ability of soils which is the capacity of soil to stay intact against the forces of erosion that come from water. This allows it to regulate the macropores, reduce the crusting of the surface, and ensures the soil is aerated, and thus reduce erosion of soil and runoff water.

It also helps for retaining organic matter inside the aggregates and shielding them from microbial contamination

Earthworms, which are huge soil organisms, produce macropores. The burrowing movement of earthworms improved the availability of nutrients as well as drainage. This leads to more stable soil structures.

The Soil Management and the Practices to improve the soil

The first of the series of actions that can help keep the soil healthy is:

1. Reduced Inversions and Soil Movement

Experts say that the presence of oxygen in soil stimulates the activity of microbial organisms and leads to degradation. Also, it alters soil the aggregates, and also exposes soil elements previously protected from the microbial attack. Organic matter should be added to soil in order to limit the regular loss of soil and to improve the health of the soil.

Tillage decreases the amount of coverage available from crop residues, which makes soil erosion more likely.

A regular tillage tool is those that include the Moldboard Plow, Disk Plow, Chisel Plow

Concept of Soil Compaction Concept of Soil Compaction

This happens when the soil is subjected to excessive foot and machine movement in wet and plastic conditions. This compresses the pores. This makes the soil more stiff and hard for roots of plants to pass through. Also, it reduces the habitat of organisms.

Non-inversion tillage can reduce the loss. If you have to use tillage it is recommended to increase the organic matter inputs such as crop residues and manure to mitigate the negative effects. Be aware of perennial forage crop rotation using annual crop rotations.

2. Increase the amount of organic matter that is used. The application of soil residues to replenish the loss of organic soil is beneficial, as is the application for cover or annual ones. Additionally, a well-balanced mixture of green and animal manure can also be a means to maintain the organic soil matter.

If you are conducting the soil fertility test make sure you include an analysis of the organic matter content.

3. Cover crops reduce erosion and the biomass that results will fall onto the soil, adding to the amount that organic material. Taproot-based crops create macropores which lessen compaction. It adds nitrogen to soil, and can also hold

nitrogen and other nutrients, which can then be eliminated due to leaching

4. Use less Pesticides This is not just a way to prevent beneficial species from dying out in large numbers, but it can also aid in preserving the natural habitat of the organisms. Farmscaping is an all-farm ecological method to increase and sustain biodiversity , which is essential to ensure the survival of beneficial organisms. You can accomplish this by using insectsary plants such as hedgerows, cover crops, hedgerows or reservoirs of water to attract the organisms that eat insect pests.

5. Rotation of crops: Different ways of rotation of crops can cause the death of soil-borne disease and pests as well as control weeds. It also reduces the excess nutrients

6. The management of nutrients, including a tactical and efficient introduction method of compost, manure and other fertilizers, is a technique that you need to master in order to regulate the level of nutrients in the soil, which will ensure the best chance of a healthy plant. Utilizing

different sources of nutrients is an excellent soil management technique.

Raised Garden Beds

If you are able to grow your crops on soil which is higher than surface, it's what is known as raised Beds. This can be achieved with an enclosure that is sought-after that is usually made from stones, wood bales of hay or repurposed objects like dressers from the past.

You may choose to install the built-in sheet metal as well as square-foot raised beds.

By using the square foot, you're splitting the space into smaller squares that are about a foot per square. It's ideal to have a densely sown vegetable garden or a productive kitchen garden. The raised beds are a good option for growing vegetables since it allows you to regulate the characteristics and quality of your soil. Six-eight inches of elevation is sufficient to accomplish this.

There's also a spiral-shaped garden and a hoop-house raised Bed which offers the benefits of a vegetable garden that can be used in all seasons and greater flexibility in gardening conditions and controlling factors like animals, weather and more.

Bed border is raised. Bed border can be a good alternative to use for land that is sloped. The beds are placed at the bottom of the slope to create an open garden.

Garden troughs A custom-designed raised bed and garden are the best ways to design your raised bed to meet your needs.

Making Compost

For a compost that is effective To have a compost that is effective, you must start by selecting your composting method that is open to the compost bin, which is tidy and secure from animals and also maintains the temperature.

You'll decide on your composter site, and no matter which one you decide to put it, the location should be sunny, flat and well-drained.

It is important to know how to alternate green layer with brown material layers as a result due to the nitrogen and carbon content of both.

Kitchen waste and other compostable materials that accumulate should be placed put in a container, maybe in the sink, to be dumped into compost bins. Food scraps in compost must be sealed with brown layers, unless you wish for to see it break down slowly and always follow instructions for compost bins from manufacturer.

You should continue to add new layers until the bin is full since it shrinks as it breaks down. Additionally, you must learn how to maintain the compost bin properly by mixing the both layers every time the addition of a new element and, if it is intended to be moist, include dry materials or water if needed and mix it every week to aid in with the process of breakdown.

The compost will be ready for harvest when it becomes dark, crumbly and has an earthy smell. This is usually 4 to six months. After you have applied the compost, ensure that you apply it at least once a year or as a top dressing for flower beds as well as the bottom of the shrubs after mixing well with the soil of your flower beds or garden. It acts as an amendment to soil; if it is possible, create the "compost tea" by filling a pillowcase with the equivalent of a liter of compost. It can be it is sprayed as required.

A few Fruit Tree and Edible Vines
There are several easy to grow and harvest varieties due to their distinctive nature and their commercial value. However you choose to plant them, whether as one tree in your backyard , or the perfect garden for it You should explore:

1. White mulberry- typically found in health stores. It's less acidic in comparison to dart-colored varieties, with a variety of varieties, including Tehama as well as the sweet lavendar.

2. Jujubeoriginated in China Its name is derived from the candy jujube and can be consumed in its raw form. They are a great choice for spindly, thorny plants with narrow upright growth and have drought

tolerance. More resilient in hot and dry conditions

3. Cider Apple- though with many varieties on the market it is possible to include one at home.

4. Pawpaw- the soft-textured fruit won't appeal to commercial growers with large scales However, they are a favourite by backyard botanists

5. Pineapple guava, often known as feijoas, can be kept in a container that can be brought insideinstead of outdoors.

6. Quinceis usually grown like you would cultivate apples and pears.

7. Loquat, A subtropical Asian fruit that has the same flavor and texture like apricots, and is best in warm climates and is unsuitable for containers for growing inside.

8. Arctic Kiwifruit- is tolerant to shade, often referred to as Arctic beauty, or even kolomikta.

9. Chocolate vineis also a shade-tolerant plant , also known as akebia. Its scent is similar to vanilla during the springtime

10. There's also Maypop and the Maypop, all of which are available for you to pick from.

Raising Backyard Chickens

If you've decided to go into poultry farming in addition to the fact that you will have to bear the smell, you'll also be taught to clean your garden, and you will be able to benefit from fresh eggs, but you should not be so busy that you don't pay attention.

It is generally recommended to have an effective plan for your Coop and then building it according to your needs or buying an already built one that can meet your needs will come in useful.

It's no harm to begin the business of raising chickens without knowing the best place to find experts locally, and you will not waste hours of wasting time diagnosing their common issues that will certainly lead you to nowhere.

Also, you must be prepared, as at the very least the chicken could die horribly and you will be shocked. It is a very tragic time is something you need to prepare for.

It is possible to include one rooster into this group. But be sure you know the proper name of each one so that you don't confuse an rooster as something else or the other way around.

You're probably wondering what happens to your chicken and eggs. Yes! They're likely to not provide eggs in the exact amount you'd like them to; it's all about patience.

Don't be upset when you begin asking questions about their health from those who are willing to listen the way you ask your child if they are suffering from certain ailments; it's normal and normal particularly in the midst of infections and illnesses.

They are dirty and smelly. I would think that this is obvious, therefore the results you'll get will depend on how you handle them.

In the case of chickens as well as eggs in your yard,, you are not starving and watching them run around with joy is more entertaining than any other animal television you could imagine.

Look for signs that the hen is no longer of utility; after two years of producing eggs the value of their eggs drops to the degree that they become an expense. You could think of selling them instead of suffer losses that could be avoided.

If you have this knowledge you'll be better ready to manage your chickens in the backyard

Plants Nutrients

Major plant nutrients originate from soil. This is mostly nitrogen, phosphorus, as well as potassium, which is referred to as NPK in plants.

Additionally, there's magnesium, calcium, and sulfur. There's also a slight requirement for zinc, magnesse as well as copper, iron and molybdenum, as well as iron which is considered to be trace elements since plants require trace amounts of it.

The nitrogen (N) is one of the vital nutrient. it is present in all plant cells, proteins hormones, as well as the chlorophyll. The atmosphere is the source of nitrogen being the main source of soil nitrogen

Chocolate soil is beneficial for plants since they have higher organic content and more nitrogen more than podzolic soil.

To prevent loss of Nitrate via leaching, make use of manure as a plant nutrients.

The phosphorus(P) transfers energy from the sun to the plant, aids in the plant to grow and start its roots.

Potassium (K) improves resistance to disease and carries starch, oil as well as sugar, to the plants

Calcium (Ca) beneficial for new hair roots and root hair growthand healthy root

Magnesium (Mg)is a significant component of chlorophyll, which helps in photosynthetic processes in the plants.

Sulfur (S)helps in the care of amino acids found in plants. proteins in plants.

The trace elements of nutrient comprise ferrous (Fe) magnesse (Mn) copper (Cu) Zinc (Zn) Boron (B) and molybdenum (Mo).

Yields of Crops

The yield of your crop is how you determine the grade of crops that are grown in the area. This will let you know whether the quality of produce is excessive or insufficient. This also aids farmers to determine the value they can earn from their produce.

It will allow you to determine the efficacy of food production relative to consumption based on the demand.

Estimating Crops Yields,

It is simply taking into account the amount of crop that can be grown on a specific space of land in the time of the year.

This is significant because it allows you to evaluate actual yield against estimated potential yield.

Also, note that the income you earn from the farm's produce depends on the volume of your production.

This is why that we pay a higher price of certain farm products in certain years, and an lower cost for the same item another year.

Pest and Disease Control

It is essential to learn how to manage this living thing that is threatening the existence of your crops on a regular basis. the pest is not just inflexible, but it is also too large in a manner that it poses a huge threat to the farmer.

The identification of the animal that caused the damage and the severity of the damage can be more challenging than you imagine.

Pest

In this category, you'll see things such as:

They are Ants, Aphids, Bay suckers of trees, Bean seeds fly, Birds, Cats, Cherry aphids(blackfly), Euonymus scale, Gall mites, Slugs Scale insects Rabbits Snails, Spider mites, Squirrelsand more.

If you are at a crossroads in your battle and are plagued, here are some items to keep in your mind.

1. It is not recommended to use too many nitrogen fertilizers as it encourages the growth of leafy plants which invite pests to your garden.

2. It is recommended to put up physical barriers to protect the crops with fleece or fruits planted in a cage.

3. Be aware of the specific bug that is causing the damage or will cause damage to your crops.

4. Be on the lookout for the first indication of an attack, and then confront it right away.

5. Make sure you follow an excellent garden hygiene routine with each device that you use to avoid any kind of disease

6. Develop better practices for cultivation that will ensure adequate watering, ample lighting and ventilation, and good soil health. This makes your crops more susceptible to be attacked.

7. The natural prey of pests to be found in the garden

8. In the last instance consider using pesticides after having a thorough understanding of the most effective application of these. For instance, chemical products are not recommended to be applied in ponds or other water habitats.

Disease

This includes the Apple scab blackleg, bacterial canker bloom wilt, botrytis and brown rot. silver leaf mushroom, tomatoes greenback etc.

Irrigation and water

Two of the most effective ways to make use of water when growing crop production are irrigation and rainwater.

Rain-fed farming refers to the process of utilize the natural rain to provide water for the soil. The benefit is that food-borne contamination items is much less probable however, you could suffer from water deficiency if rainfall is reduced.

Irrigation is an unnatural application of water to the soil, generally using various types of equipment such as pumps, sprays and tubes. The use of irrigation is usually to enhance the effect of intermittent rain. As an agriculturalist, you need choose the most suitable source for your irrigation water supplyto reduce or limit the possibility of contamination.

Types of Irrigation Systems

There are many ways to apply the water you have on your farm, however you need to choose the most efficient method in accordance with your requirements and the characteristics of the crops. A few of these strategies are listed below:

1. Surface irrigation: You will spray water on the ground via gravity. You don't require any pump mechanical.

2. Localized irrigation - you spray water through a pipes of low pressure to plants.

3. Drip irrigationis an irrigation method that is localized in which you place water at the roots of plants in order to minimize runoff and evaporation.

4. Sprinkler irrigation sprays water over the top of the farm with a high-pressure sprinklers from a central location in the farm, or from moving platform

5. Center pivot irrigationis done in a circular fashion by sprinklers that move through wheeled towers. It is best for flat terrains.

6. Lateral move irrigation water gets into the farm through a number of pipes that have wheels, and sprinklers, which can be

turned manually or by a constructed method; less expensive however labor-intensive.

7. Sub-irrigation-pumping stations, canals, etc. utilize raised water tables that disperse water throughout the entire farm.

8. Manual irrigation - as the name suggests the water is sprayed manually across the ground using containers for watering; it is also labor-intensive.

How to Begin Seeds

You'll learn about the many methods to successfully plant your seeds. But remember that each plant's seed is different and should be treated as such by using the correct lighting and the right equipment, you are able to prepare seeds starting at that stage until harvest time. Start with a the tomato varieties which are simple to grow indoors.

These are the stages of this vital procedure:

1. You need to be able to predict when it isThe main objective is to plant seeds in

the time of a favorable environment therefore by studying the seeds' labels you'll be able to recognize the proper method to handle seeds. Because certain seeds are most suitable for outdoor cultivation, while some do not.

2. Find the correct Can to use it- every container should be between 3 and 4 inches of depth with a type of drainage holes can be used to start seeds according to the requirements, however there are specially designed trays for seeds to ensure consistent water.

3. Then, you will mix the potting soil. Make sure to use potting soil that is made for seedlings that are developing; Perhaps, you can begin with a new sterile mix that can give healthy seedlings. Make sure to water the plant mix thoroughly prior to lining the container firmly with soil so that it doesn't take up too much the space. The seeds generally require artificial nutrients. Perhaps you could make use of a liquid fertilizer within a couple of weeks following germination and until the transplantation of the seed occurs.

4. It is possible to begin planting however, before doing this, make sure to check the directions regarding how deep or shallow the particular seed can be planted. It is well-known that smaller seeds can be sprinkled onto the surface of the soil and larger ones are usually placed deep in the soil. Seeds that are newly planted require moisture to accelerate the process of germination, so it is recommended to add some water using the aid of a watering container. You can cover seeding pots with a plastic covering but you must take it off once the green signal of germination has been observed.

5. Feed it water then repeat the processThis is an extremely important element that determines whether the seed will grow or dies off. The process will be a periodic check , which involves irrigation to keep the soil wet. Make sure to keep a fan on to keep the surrounding well-ventilated; and provide regular food to your seedlings by using liquid fertilizer to the recommended dosage.

6. Lightis essential element to the growth of seeds; when you determine the best place to put the pot's base in the direction of the sun's entry point and making sure that the plant doesn't tilt towards the sun and you'll be sure to get an enlightened seed. If you are growing under lighting, they must only be a few inches higher than the top that the seeds are growing. The light should be timed so that it reflects the normal night and day pattern. Up about 15 to 20 hours light per day is acceptable since seedlings require darkness, just as they do. The light will be extended further as it gets bigger.

7. Be careful when moving your seeds outside-from an environment that is controlled and gradually transfer the seeds from these conditions to the garden in a totally different climate. It is necessary to shade them from the sun's heat for a few hours before bringing to the indoors at night for a period of for up to 10 days. Increase the exposure gradually as they become familiar with the sun and windy conditions.

Be on the lookout for these signs when you are starting your Seed

If you notice that smaller percentage of seeds than you expected developed, it could be an indication that you didn't apply the correct temperature, light or similar. Make sure that the soil is dry and cold than you expected. It is possible to uproot a seed and then determine whether a rot has occurred. Watch for a tender and swollen indicator of mold.

If there is excessive drying in the soil then the seed may have dried out rather than sprout.

If you find that your seeds have grown spindly, that's another indication that they didn't get the necessary hours of light It could be the result of high temperatures as well. The correction of the light and temperature imbalance will resolve this.

If the leaves turn a shade of purple this indicates that the the phosphorus levels are not sufficient change between full strength and half strength fertilizers will fix this issue.

Do your seeds suddenly wilt due to an unidentified reason? It could be due to an invasive plant-borne fungal infection (damping off) which is a tough fungus to eradicate and you can switch to a soilless, sterile medium that has adequate ventilation.

There is a small amount of that there is a little mold on the surface of your soil Your planting medium is likely to be wet, and you should rectify it before it begins impacting the seeds. Some things you can do include increasing ventilation and holding water back for days, or transferring the seedling's soil.

Extension of the Growing Season

While some remain stuck in the traditional growing season some are learning to extend their seasons, benefiting from the benefits of a season harvest. It's not magical, but it is a trick that only a few people know. In order to succeed, you need to:

1. Know the microclimate that is present on your farm. The best method to achieve

this is to gather your own observations of the patterns of weather and possibly the amount of rainfall that is happening in the area. even so you may not make the right decision. Therefore, it is best to stay with crops that do exceptionally well in your locale but also taking into consideration the fact that certain areas of your farm might be more exposed to scorching heat than others due to shade of trees, fences and so on. Knowing this information will assist you in choosing the most effective strategy.

2. It is important to plant regularly. is a great way to do this. After you've transplanted seeds from the seedlings you started then you'll start another seed to follow in the same order. Additionally, vegetables thrive in different seasons, so you could plant the best suited to the conditions now and then plant a few weeks later. And as you harvest your first crops then you'll be introducing another variety to the soil based on its cold and hot weather requirements.

3. You can also plant multiple varieties of plants with different maturities This way you can harvest your crops in a consistent manner, each one following the next when each one matures.

4. Get rid of weeds as early and thoroughly. Vegetables like tomatoes, for instance, can are able to grow quickly in a less crowded garden You're aware that weeds can challenge crops in a detrimental way thus removing them as soon as you can, at minimum, every two weeks.

5. You could decide to put in raised beds in your garden. This is a great idea to improve the health of the plants, particularly because turning the soil appears to increase the number of weeds, Therefore, raised beds can result in less work.

6. Use Trellises. This makes it simpler to control the growth of weeds in the root of the plant

7. You can adopt inter-planting-combining compatible veggies in the same row show a lot of benefits; planting fast growth ones

with slower ones, and hot weather plants with cold ones: with one acting as a shade, do not only ensures more regular harvest, it's also healthy to the plants.

8. Rotating crops - shifting the position of your crops of the same variety within the same soil from one specific season of planting to another. It makes sure that you don't utilize the same soil over two seasons, within rows for the same reason. This increases the capacity of the soil to produce larger and produce more.

9. Only apply artificial water whenever it is necessary. Unless you tell us otherwise stated, most gardens will benefit from regular rain as excessive water could cause roots to sink on the soil's surface rather than sink downwards. It's not necessarily your fault, however it is important to be aware of this to ensure that it is efficient. Make sure you water as early as you can prior to sunset to allow the water to dry in the afternoon's warm sun.

10. Be aware of early frost. Try to eliminate this with sheeting made of plastic or old bed sheets in the event that

you'll take it off during sunny days to prevent excessive heat, and take care to not break the plants stems when doing this.

11. You can create a Cold frame to protect specific crops that are frequently affected by minor variations in the weather. The rectangular, shallow bottom with a clear plastic top will encase the sun's warming rayons. The primary goal in the design of the box is to make sure that your winter vegetables will grow in summer to harvest during winter, for example.

12. Start seeds indoors. Starting seeds indoors allows you to plan prior to purchasing from the usual supply.

13. Also, you should plant the seeds at a sufficient time in particular if you're working with raised beds for getting your plants until the soil in your garden is able to take the seeds. A soil thermometer is useful for assessing the soil's condition without or with the raised beds to ensure healthy plants.

14. Make sure that the plants are protected from late frosts and design for

success, if you have to succeed in this region.

How to preserve your harvest

If you've successfully harvested your crops, and that you have plenty; you should be aware of how to preserve your harvest to ensure that you continue to profit from it at any time. In accordance with what you intend to keep there are many ways to store it, one of which I've identified in the following:

1. Storing fresh vegetables. Items like cabbages, carrots and so on. can be a means of staying fresh as long as they are properly preserved. Certain crops can remain fresh for up to 6 months.

It is important to know that although some fruits and vegetables can be preserved by an icy and humid environment, other produce will remain fresh and fresher in a quiet dry and dry environment. Be sure to ensure that rodents are kept away. The storage type and the contents to be stored should be considered when deciding on storage facilities.

2. Freezing-freezers are an extremely useful tool to preserve. If handled properly, some vegetables and fruits can keep their original flavor as well as color and nutritional value when compared to other storage methods; however, it is recommended not to freeze the fresh crop with high water content such as cucumbers.

3. Freezer Jam If you've got the skills, you can create an freezer Jam made with berries. It's not just fun, but also it's also a lot easier than cooking jams. Be sure to read the directions regarding how to make the freezer jams prior to making them and it's crucial.

4. Pesto- After making the most delicious pesto in an excellent blender, it is possible to freeze up to one year and is easy to prepare using the proper containers.

5. Water bath canning is particularly useful during an extended power cut, which is great to preserve acidic fruits such as apples and berries. To make this process efficient you will require an canning kettle with the rack and lid along with a jar lifter,

as well as large mouth funnels; Also, self-sealing lids and jars. It's possible that you need to learn a tutorial on how to can. It's also crucial.

6. Salsa-making salsa is an activity that will be a lot of fun, particularly in the event that you have plenty of tomatoes and other fruits after harvest. There is also an entire guide to salsa recipes. It is also possible to store it in the freezer for months.

7. Picking-if you already own a water bath canner it's much easier to use vinegar's strength as a preservative on your fruits. Shelf-safe pickles. They don't require an extended fermentation time.

8. Pressure canning - low acid food items like corn have to undergo this type of process to last longer. The primary goal of this is to eliminate, for example the botulism-causing bacteria when temperatures are at 250 ° F or higher.

9. Dry Herbsis the process of stringing clean, unsprayed herb stems using strings before placing their upside down into a humid but dehydrated part of the house.

The length of time required to dry is contingent on the kind of herb used and the humidity of the area in which it was stored in.

10. Vine dried beans is as easy as drying the beans during sunny weather. If you need to an oven or dehydrators will be useful. The beans will be stored in bags for 48hrs before storing the beans.

11. Dehydratingmeans simply removing the water to keep fruit, for example, fresh and dry.

Additionally, you can make use of Flavored Vinegar Fermenting, fermenting, alcohol Infusions as well as Craft Wine and Cider; to preserve your harvest.

Chapter 9: The Different Types Of Gardening Based On The Space

It's not required to have the identical amount of space to what I do. It is therefore essential to think about your space and alter the space accordingly to your needs so that you can utilize the space effectively. If you're just beginning with your new garden the most difficult task in your face is deciding what you'll do to modify the space in relation to the initial use of vegetables, while also preserving the life of your soil. The protection and preservation of the soil's natural resources is the basis to organic farming. Here are some different types of organic farming you can pick based on the area you have and other aspects:The following are the most common:

1. The Backyard Organic Garden Organic backyard edible gardens are best for the initial space of 20X5 square feet. The typical timeframe for this kind of garden is around 2-4 weeks. You can utilize mulch, newspaper and compost to do this kind of gardening. The most important benefit of

this kind of garden is that you are able to maintain your garden on your own without the need for a second person's assistance. I had a clean lawn that was gently sloped. I had the idea of growing some edible fruit trees and berries in this particular garden. I knew I wanted to recreate a nutritious dense forest floor over a brief amount of time, so I chose an approach to soil layering known as lasagna gardening in which I used newspapers along with compost, as well as some mulch. I started the process in beginning of spring before grass was growing and laid the grass down with 10 layers of newspaper. I overlapping the papers in order that grass wouldn't be able to get through. I then lightly moistening the paper before covering them with mulch and compost.

I waited about a month before planting flowers, berry bushes, pollinator-attracting perennials, and veggies in each garden. The grass and the newspaper decayed and made it simple to cut. The area was awash with soil organic matter and worms in the beginning and stays the same way, with mulch and compost. This method is possible to use however, you must read this entire book to know how to cultivate compost, as well as other techniques for organic mini-farming before implementing this method.

2. Organic Market GardenAfter I got used to the traditional method of gardening within smaller spaces, I decided to try an organic market garden where the size of your first site is 100X50 square feet. The duration of this type of garden is about one month. You are able to cultivate winter squash and potatoes in this kind of garden. The tools you will need to need are a mower broadfork, rototiller manure forks, rake 1 helper and compost.

I picked this method to implement this method with the idea that it could allow a person to expand their space of garden to production in a short time. Following the first tillage there's been no additional work related to growing potatoes. The best time to begin is in the middle of April, when soil is able to be working. Cut the grass as short as much as you can and do a couple of slow passes using the help of a Rototiller. After a week, visit the spot with a broadfork for deep rooting of the sod. Perform a regular pass using your rototiller, and your soil will be prepared to plant potatoes.

It is important to consider the level of nutrients available in this particular garden because of the quantity of organic matter decaying. You can add soil to the rows before planting to control this issue. It is also possible to grow winter squash and oil radish among the rows that are spaced widely to achieve the same situation.

3. Community Garden SiteThis type of garden is also suitable for tiny spaces of 20x40 square feet. The timeframe for the garden community site is between 7 and 10 days. The most important resources to help with this kind of gardening are Sod cutters that are rented and shovels, rototillers, shovels compost manure, and a few assistance. The garden location due to its sun-filled location and the potential for

growth. Take the sod off of your garden which would take approximately two hours. It is possible to use this sod to compost your garden too. Double dug your garden , and apply manure throughout the area. Rototillers are a great way to incorporate the manure. The site is ready to plant.

4. Space Foot GardeningI'd tried the three previous methods of gardening in my garden , where it was soil. But I also wanted plant some plants in my backyard that was solid, and also some planters on my roof as well. I decided to go with the method of square foot gardening, where you can utilize any space such as your roof or in your backyard for gardening. It is possible to use any space that is suitable for the size of your roof and backyard when you are gardening this way. This is a list of the most essential materials for gardening:

A) A few wood boards (150X44mm) depending on your preference of gardening.

B) Pine planks 6X1200 to use as cover strips.

C) Set screws of 9 hexagons.

D) Chipboard 16 and 12, screws with smooth shanks.

E) Compost or peat moss, and palm peat.

F) A trellis-like panel (1000x1200mm)

G) Plastic

H) 20 nails

I) Electric drill with screwdriver attachment.

J) Hammer

K) Flat 16mm and ringspanner.

(l) Spade, hand trowel and rake.

Follow this step by procedure to create an area of square feet for a garden in your neighborhood:--

A) Make three 6 mm openings at the end from each pine board at a distance of 22 millimeters from the edge.

b) Take the sheets and arrange them in an elongated square and fix them using the 6x75 mm screws into the gaps.

C) Spread the bottom of the system using plastic and attach it to the an area using the nails for tack.

D) Select a place to place your growing box which is level, free from trees and bushes with root systems that are intrusive, and receives 5 to 6 hours of sunlight each day. Be aware of any trees and structures that might cause shadows to be cast over it especially during winter when the intensity of the sun's rays is more compressed.

E) Remove any grass and weeds in the area you have picked.

F) Make your own dirt mix by combining equivalent quantities of manure that is great and peat greenery (or palm peat) and vermiculite measured in volume and not weight. The quality of the soil is crucial to this kind of growing and you must not revert to it or you'll smell it in your green products. It is best to build your own soil mix. The vermiculite and peat give excellent drainage while retaining dampness and the manure provides additional nutrients.

G) The crate should be filled with 33% deepness using your dirt mix. Then, water it thoroughly. Rehash the process (filling with water) 3 times till the container is fully filled. The dirt will begin to settle as you go so you should wait for at least 1 hour before filling.

h) Put the six strips in the crate with the intention of having it divided into 16 equal squares. The strips should be secured to the sides using 4x30 millimeter screws. Cut 6 mm gaps in the strips at points where they meet and join them by using set screws with 9 hexagons as well as nuts (6x25 millimeters) scattered pieces.

I) Attach the trellis to the rear of the case to allow trailing plants by using the remaining four (6x75 mm) screws.

Different kinds of seeds for Your Organic Garden

Seeds are the primary prerequisite for organic farming. It is essential to select organic seeds if they are they are available. Pick organic seeds that are not going to be modified genetically or treated using fungicides. Here are some definitions of the different types of seeds that can assist you in selecting them:

1. Heirloom seeds or heritage Seeds which have been used in traditional agriculture for over 75 years ago are known as heirloom or heritage seeds.

2. Pollinated by open pollination:Seeds that have been been saved from a plant that has been pollinated by other plants of the same type. Pollination is natural and seeds yield vegetables with similar characteristics to the parent vegetables. These kinds of seeds are ideal for organic farming.

3. Cross pollinated seedsCross pollination is a process whereby two varieties of plants are cultivated close to each to ensure that pollination happens through natural sources such as insects and winds. The seeds that are taken from the plant will grow into a vegetable with characteristics of both varieties.

4. Hybrid seeds: seeds with mixed parentage which are designed and developed by breeders are known as hybrid seeds. They are pollinated by hand by transferring pollen from one type of plant, resulting in the new type of. Hybrid

plants are suitable for extreme weather conditions and in some regions where certain kinds of diseases are more damaging to plants. You should consider a hybrid if you feel that the weather and the disease issue is more severe in your local area.

5. Genetically modified seed:Genetic modification is the process of taking genes from various organisms like plants and bacteria and then incorporates them directly into cells of different species. Avoid these seeds since they're expensive and a certain business practices are not ethical to modify genetics.

How to enrich your soil for organic farming
I've mentioned before within this publication that the soil is the primary component of your organic farming. You should be careful to protect its natural qualities and supply it with the most nutrients naturally. The soil's biological elements often are not noticed within the gardens. It is essential to know the function of soil and the living organisms it

hosts in organic agriculture. The conventional farming system has damaged the natural attributes of our soil since they do not care about any negative impacts to our bodies. Their primary goal is to produce foodstuffs in abundance in order to make it affordable and accessible to cultivate. The green revolution has been focused on the soil's chemical composition, such as nitrogen, Phosphorus, and potassium. However, if you're organically-oriented it is necessary to adopt an entirely different approach to farming. The primary goal of organic farming is to maintain and build the soil's biological diversity.

Building Healthy Soils

There are some issues to be faced when you have small gardens in order to ensure soil structure and create organic matter. It is necessary to overburden the soil with weed-inducing nutrients. Many vegetable gardeners tend to favor adding manure which is thought to be a highly soluble nutrient to the soil, which could lead to an over-fertilization on the gardening plot.

Consider the following factors to avoid fertilizing too much: -

1. Make use of crop rotation
2. Make the soil work to increase the quality of its life
3. Make use of organic matter as often as you can, such as organic compost and mulch. or cover plants that are naturally grown within your home.
4. Don't over fertilize and don't make use of fertilizers made with chemicals.
5. Only add manure after you're certain that your soil needs it and only if you are certain that the manure source is organic

Making Organic Compost for your Organic Farm

Your compost requires proper monitoring and maintenance to ensure proper decomposition. Finding the best methods for most efficient compost production can be a long process, however there are many methods you can employ in your composting to ensure that the process is efficient and efficient. Here are a few strategies for compost gardening These are:

Location

The ideal location where you can compost is in direct sunlight. The sun's rays dry the compost heap and direct exposure to the high winds can dry and cool the pile. It is also possible to put the pile of compost on soil that has drainage systems that are well-designed to prevent excessive water. Don't place our pile on top of a wooden structure or tree as it gets in contact with compost can cause decay. It is also possible to consider other considerations placing your pile in the middle from garden and lawn activities close to water sources, or in places where there is enough space to store organic wastes.

Volume

The amount of compost you put in is also an important notion for good growth and development of microorganisms within your compost. Your compost heap must be large enough to hold heat , but not enough to allow air to get to the middle. The minimum size for your compost heap is 3X3X3 feet . It should not exceed the limit of 5ftX5ft by any length. If the compost pile is smaller than the size of a cubic yard it is recommended to insulate your sides. If the pile is larger than 5 feet it is necessary to rotate the material frequently in order to increase the flow of air and prevent anaerobic activities.

Pile Construction

The most effective method to build a compost pile is to mix the ingredients in small batches as they become usable. If you wish to make your compost to be more efficient and have enough greens and browns, you can build your compost by layering the two types of material in approximately 4-6 inches increments. Continue mixing each layer as you mix substances. The pile you have created should be composted more quickly than a simple mess. If you don't dispose of a lot of garbage, you can layer the items you've added when more is available. This technique is slower than batch pile however it is the most popular method employed by a lot of small-sized homes.

Maintenance of the Pile

The care of the compost pile is an crucial aspect to consider for the best compost gardening. The amount of maintenance required completely dependent on the person Simply turning the mountain at least every week is suggested. Many people do the turning and adding simultaneously, which integrates the new materials faster. Sometimes, adding water is required, but simply turning the pile can help to distribute the moisture more effectively.

Your compost pile is finished when it reaches 10deg F at ambient temperature, and then decreases by about 1/3rd of its original volume. Your compost must be dark with a pleasant odor and should not have any visible leftovers of ingredients that have been partially decomposed.

Pest Avoidance

Pests do not benefit your compost heap and it is important to stay clear of any compost material that can attract rodents and pests like fish and meat scraps bones, cheeses, butter and other dairy and meat products. Food items like clams, and others which contain an abundance of sugars and sugars can attract insects, so stay clear of these items as much as you move them away. If your country is experiencing an extensive problem with rodents and other pests, you could purchase an industrial bin that can be used for compost. This will stop the large rodents from entering. The use of completed compost or carbonated material like straw could help with the pest control.

Health-related Considerations

It is important to take care of health concerns when the composting process. It is a good idea to wash your hands after playing to prevent any illness. The normal allergic reaction can occur often because of an abundance of mold or the fungi that live in compost. If you suffer an allergy of any kind you should apply an allergen-related dustmark during cleaning, composting and then turn the pot.

Different kinds of composting systems

There are a variety of composting methods that are being widely used by a variety of gardeners and farmers in the present. You can choose the most effective method based on your preference and the ease of use. Here are a few of the most efficient compost gardening methods for youto choose from:

Hot Compost System

Hot compost systems are generally large enough to produce a lot of heat that kills disease-causing weeds and plants within the compost. Hot compost is in the category of "batch process systems" because you have to combine all the necessary equipment and ingredients in the beginning of the process in a single step. Then, you have to reverse the process to ensure that the higher temperature will fill every crevice of your compost pile. The hot compost produces a temperature between 55 and 65 degrees Celsius that's enough to flush off all harmful weeds, bacteria and seeds that are in the soil and improve the quality of your garden. Hot composting is the fastest and most pleasant method for those who don't have the time for compost gardening. It is easy to start your garden in a matter of minutes when you're planning to create an entirely new garden. If your yard isn't very large, you could make use of the trash that you have at home to create compost pile. If you're planning an extensive area of your backyard, you could purchase clippings from lawn movers. Some companies can send clippings free of charge and charge only for the cost savings.

Cold Compost System

Another popular composting system is the cold compost system. These systems of compost are utilized with plastic bins. Cold compost is likely to be the best choice in the event that you're interested in the creation of a small gardening space for the family. Kitchen waste, garden weeds, prunings, and other materials to create compost in a medium-sized compost bin. While it does warm the compost, it does not get particularly hot which is why it's described as a the cold compost method. The Cold composting system generally doesn't eliminate weeds, and it can are able to make use of another option for removing the weeds.

Indoor Vermicomposting System

Vermicomposting indoors is also popular with small-scale gardeners who only require a small amount of compost to their gardens. Vermicomposting differs from conventional composting in the way that the heap is managed to ensure that the conditions favor the worms. Worm composting bins can be found in various sizes and shapes. Worms are able to live wherever they are satisfied and some are very creative in designing worm bins. I've seen some very intricate worm bins on the internet. Whatever style you choose to choose, keep in mind the fundamentals. Make sure you are maintaining the correct temperature to allow your composting worms. Bedding should not exceed 12 inches in depth. Keep the worms moist but not wet.

Systems for stacking worms for worms are extremely popular due to their worms-to-space ratio. They are made up of composting worms and travel a extremely little space. The worm composting bins are made to accommodate the natural upward motion that worms undergo.

The systems consist of 3, 4 or 5 interlocking tray in depth, allowing the worms to stay unaffected while you harvest vermicompost. The basic principle is composting worms naturally move upwards towards their new food and litter. When they have all migrated into the holes of every tray collect the remaining castings from each tray(s) below and put the tray that is empty on the top of the stack.

Here's the listing of some of the essential components for composting Here are some of the essential materials for making compost:

1. Two reasonably-sized containers.

2. 1 part green material such as green grass or kitchen scraps from vegetables, or even green plant cuttings, etc.

3. 2 parts brown dry materials such as straw, sawdust or newspaper shredded.

4. 1/10th portion of rough material such as small sticks.

5. Sprinkles such as limestone, wood ash and organic compost activater.

How do you go about Plantation for Your Organic Farm?

Plan your plants ahead of time to ensure more accurate outcomes and greater yields. Planting companion plants (discussed in the next section) for the best results in your backyard. Companion plants help hold the soil's nutrients and keep away harmful insects. Be sure to follow the guidelines for planning which is usually a part of the seeds you're sown. You should plant the food plants you like to eat and cook with.

Some common tips for choosing Your Plants

The kind of plant you intend to sow to grow organically usually is dependent on the temperature and weather conditions. I have included a list in the next section of different plants you can plant in various seasons. But, I'd suggest you to plant twice the amount of plants in the autumn and winter months as in comparison to the quantity in the spring and summer months. The plants grow slower during winter and autumn months and the harvest are less frequent. Select the plant that best meets the needs of your family and plant enough to satisfy the needs of your family. Some crops have a brief harvest time, and you can plant a succession of plants to ensure you have enough amount of food and harvest staggered. Many of the vegetables you grow from seeds can take 4 to 6 weeks to mature when compared to transplanting seeds. If you're growing your own seedlings start 4 to 6 weeks prior to the desired season for plants.

Do not plant the same plants or plants from the same household as they will deplete the soil of essential nutrients and promote soil-borne pests. You can, for instance, plant tomatoes, legumes squash, and corn during an annual rotation of four years. You could also employ the companion planting technique to your garden, something I've discussed in a different section of this book in order to preserve the natural nutrients within your garden. It's not an issue if you're employing square foot gardening as you can move the soil with this plan. You can plant small varieties when you have an area of only a few square feet or choose varieties that can be planted in a vertical manner on an tree.

A few plants for the Spring and Summer months.

1. Pepper, Pumpkin, or Runner beans, Cucumber, Marrows, Sweet potatoes, Rhubarb, melons: 1 plant per square per trellis.
2. Turnips, leeks, and lettuce Four each.
3. Beetroot as well as spinach. Swiss Chard nine plants in a square.
4. Carrots, celery, and radishes sixteen plants in a square.

Some plants to enjoy Autumn and Winter

1. Broccoli, broad beans peas, cabbages, cauliflower one plant in each square trellis.

2. Leeks, lettuce, turnips Four each.

3. Beetroot and spinach Swiss Chard Nine plants for each square.

4. Carrots onion, celery, carrots sixteen plants in a square.

Watering A cup of water around the root of each plant in the mid-morning time. It is also possible to use an irrigation system that drips for those who require.

Companion Planting

Companion gardening is a method to grow one or more varieties of plants within a garden. There are many advantages of companion gardening , such as preserving vital nutrients, preventing pests and attracting insects to aid in pollinating plants. Did you know that basil and tomatoes seem as if they were made for each other and do very well when they are together? A lot of farmers are now able to cultivate certain plants as they are a good match and this is not only beneficial to the plants but also beneficial to the ecosystem and the natural world. The plants are able to help each other in a variety of ways, such as fighting insects, releasing substances that release nutrients or provide shelter to one another. Planting companion plants is ideal for your mini-farming that is edible since you will save costs of using plant food and pesticides.

Here are some possible combinations of companion plants that you could use:--

1. Garlic and roses
2. The cabbage and tomatoes
3. Peppers and the pigweed
4. Lettuce and large flowers
5. Spinach and radishes
6. Melons and Marigolds
7. Sweet potatoes and potatoes Alyssum

Certain plants repel pests

Certain plants have fragrant foliage which makes it difficult for pests relying on their sense of smell to locate their plants of prey. If you are able to plant these plants in your garden along with other plants, you can prevent pests from harming your efforts in the orchard. You can plant lavender and tansy as well as rosemary, thyme and mint as well as Alyssum to repel pests in your garden for edibles.

Some plants that draw beneficial insects that pollinate

Pollination is the process through which the grains of flowers of the male plant are transferred onto the female stigma the plant. Pollination is necessary by many plants in order to produce seeds and fruits. Today, on the other side are insects including butterflies, bees and butterflies which aid in pollination of plants, making it important for your garden's edible. There are pollen-producing plants such as daisies, borage and roses, as well as lavender sunflowers, fresh peas, and yarrow in order to attract worms that aid in pollination.

A few Natural Soil and Plant Doctors

Remember that you're doing tiny farming on your property to protect yourself from the harmful chemicals and pesticides that are used for commercial farming. Your next priority is to make use of organic pesticides to your edible garden. Camomile is a plant that is famous as a plant doctor due to its many benefits to other plants. It stimulates the growth and growth of various plants. It and has aromatic leaves that repel pests and insects and has a significant calcium content within its leaves. Lime is crucial to maintain the pH within your soil. Its leaves may be used as green manure or as compost.

The Control of Pests and Insects in your Mini Farm Naturally
Pest control is essential to the majority of plants you grow in organic farming to ensure their optimal growth. You can apply these easy steps to manage unwanted insects and pests in your garden.

1. Combine 2 teaspoons soap-based liquid detergent that is made from an organic source (avoid the phosphate-based version) together with 1 gallon water. Then spray it onto your plants. The soap spray can be effective in fighting aphids.

2. Make a small amount of diatomaceous and sprinkle it all over your plants. Diatomaceous is a powder that has been fossilized of sea creatures from the past

which can prevent the development of snails and snails which are harmful to your plants. If diatomaceous is not readily available in your region, you can use crushed egg shells to do similar purposes. Egg shells provide calcium to soil that can be beneficial to plants.

3. You can rotate your crop every year and switch planting locations to maintain the nutritional quality of the soil in your garden.

4. Create a variety of varieties of plants within your yard. Pests are a problem when there isn't enough variety of plants in the garden.

5. Don't use pesticides that are harmful to your health since they could destroy beneficial bugs in your garden. These insecticides are unhealthy for humans.

Homemade Pesticides to Use in Your Rooftop Garden

Conclusion

Thank you for buying this book.

I hope that it's served as a helpful introduction to square foot and indoor gardening, and has encouraged you to plant your own garden.

There is something incredibly satisfying about growing your own vegetables. this makes it simpler and less time-consuming. Furthermore, the vegetables are more delicious and can never be fresher It's an all-win for everyone.

Children of all ages enjoy playing with dirt, and watch the things develop. It's an amazing moment cook something you created from scratch and also to give the bounty to your family and friends.

Happy gardening!

www.ingramcontent.com/pod-product-compliance
Lightning Source LLC
Chambersburg PA
CBHW050406120526
44590CB00015B/1848